Without Reservations

The Cartoons of RICARDO CATÉ

GIBBS SMITH

TO ENRICH AND INSPIRE HUMANKIND

In memory of Joe and Crucita Caté (grandparents on dad's side), Lucy M. Garcia (my mom's mother) and Juan Caté (my dad).

First Edition
22 21 20   10 9 8 7

Published by
Gibbs Smith
P.O. Box 667
Layton, Utah 84041

1.800.835.4993 orders
www.gibbs-smith.com

Designed by Andrew Brozyna
Printed and bound in Hong Kong
Gibbs Smith books are printed on either recycled, 100% post-consumer waste, FSC-certified papers or on paper produced from sustainable PEFC-certified forest/controlled wood source. Learn more at www.pefc.org.

ISBN: 978-1-4236-3009-8

"How many times do American Indians see their portrayals in the mainstream media? Not many. And, conversely, how many times do we get to see ourselves portrayed in the mainstream media when we know we are being 'poked fun at,' by one of our own? Sadly, not very often, unless you are located in one of the media markets that publish Ricardo Caté's, *Without Reservations*. Without sounding overly masochistic, here in Santa Fe we are lucky enough to see Ricardo's daily reminders of life in Indian Country and can go about our day after having laughed mightily, snorted in disgust, or just shrugged our shoulders and said 'huh?' to one of his daily captioned scenes of Indian on Indian, or Indian on Whiteman, the reverse, or any combination thereof. Caté's cartoons serve to remind us there is always a different point of view for any situation, such as being able to gauge a horse's age by the number of teeth marks a horse can make on a cowboy's butt after having bitten the boy, or everyday scenes of home life where Indian kids act just like their brethren of different races. *Without Reservations* is always thought-provoking whether it makes you laugh, smirk, or just enjoy the diversity of thought to be found in Indian Country."

—*Wes Studi,*
Cherokee actor

"Caté is a funny guy. This is to say, that the reality of Native America is both tragic and hilarious . . . this experience needs a satirist . . . Caté is our man. For those of us entrenched in the greatness and depth of our communities, we find that his heart- and gut-felt humor speaks to our minds, memories, and hearts."

—*Winona LaDuke, Anishinaabekwe (Ojibwe) activist,*
environmentalist, economist and writer

INTRODUCTION

I grew up with my grandparents on the Santo Domingo Reservation during assimilation. It is traditionally known as Santo Domingo Pueblo (the Spanish explorers gave it that name) then some activists changed it to "kewa," which is its indigenous name. It is located between Santa Fe and Albuquerque along I-25 (exit 259).

My parents worked in Albuquerque, and I was fortunate that I didn't grow up in the city at that time. Except for high school, college, and the Marine Corps, I've always lived near home. I went to high school in Ignacio, Colorado on the Southern Ute Indian Reservation where the Indian students who boarded there were bussed to a public high school just half a mile away. I then attended Allen Community College in Iola, Kansas for two years on a running scholarship (cross-country and track). I tried the University of New Mexico for a year, but joined the Marine Corps, where I was stationed in Japan for the first two years and Camp Pendleton in California the last two. Right now I deal cards at San Felipe's Casino Hollywood and teach GED courses at the pueblo. I have also worked as a public school teacher teaching 7th to 8th grade social

> I hope that my cartoons are successful in marketing to all races and ethnicities. I like to think that this is a universal cartoon in which the characters just happen to be Native, although there are specific messages I like to get across that concern Native Americans.

studies. Other odd jobs have included: construction, dishwashing, security guard, laborer, bartender, and even Avon sales rep for a couple of months! I will do anything I can to support my family.

I get my sense of humor from my dad, uncles, and my brothers and their relentless teasing and joking around. I started drawing cartoons with my best friend David in 7th grade. We drew cartoons about everything: ourselves, our teachers, and our friends doing everyday school stuff. Most of the time we were the only ones who got the jokes from our cartoons, so we knew we had a unique sense of humor. We read every *MAD* magazine issue that came out (Don Martin was my favorite and I always wished I could draw like him). It was then that I became more aware of my surroundings and started to see the humor in everyday life at school, home, and even in church.

Today, my cartoons are featured in daily newspapers such as *The Santa Fe New Mexican*. People from my community/tribe really enjoy my cartoons and they always "get it," while their non-Native counterparts have a hard time understanding some of them. I've learned to make the jokes more universal.

There are those who say my cartoons aren't politically correct. I would say to them that they could pick up any history or social studies textbook and find political incorrectness in the chapters dealing with Native Americans. Maybe that's a bit extreme. If people aren't willing to accept my views and insights as a Native American living in this country, then maybe I won't accept Garfield's views and insights as a cat living in this country!

I am not a spokesman for any tribe. I am simply drawing the funny side to what I know and experience as a Native in this country. I hope this book will once again put my village of Santo Domingo on the map. We have been known for my people's handcrafted jewelry as well as our pottery. We, unfortunately, also have an unemployment rate of 48 percent, and there are young adults wishing to further their education to help change that statistic. However, there aren't enough funds to help these young adults, so if the book is successful, I would very much like to help these kids finish their education so that they, in turn, can give back to our community.

Ricardo's Top Five Favorite Comics
1. Don Martin (from *MAD* magazine)
2. Calvin and Hobbes (Bill Watterson)
3. Peanuts (Charles Schultz)
4. Garfield (Jim Davis)
5. Without Reservations (Ricardo Caté)

> **Sometimes I get letters from non-Natives who have called me racist and insensitive to Natives until they realize that I am Native myself. Non-Natives often walk up to me and say, "I didn't *get* the cartoon today," and I reply, "That's ok, I don't get the cartoons in *The New Yorker* either."**

THE CARTOONS

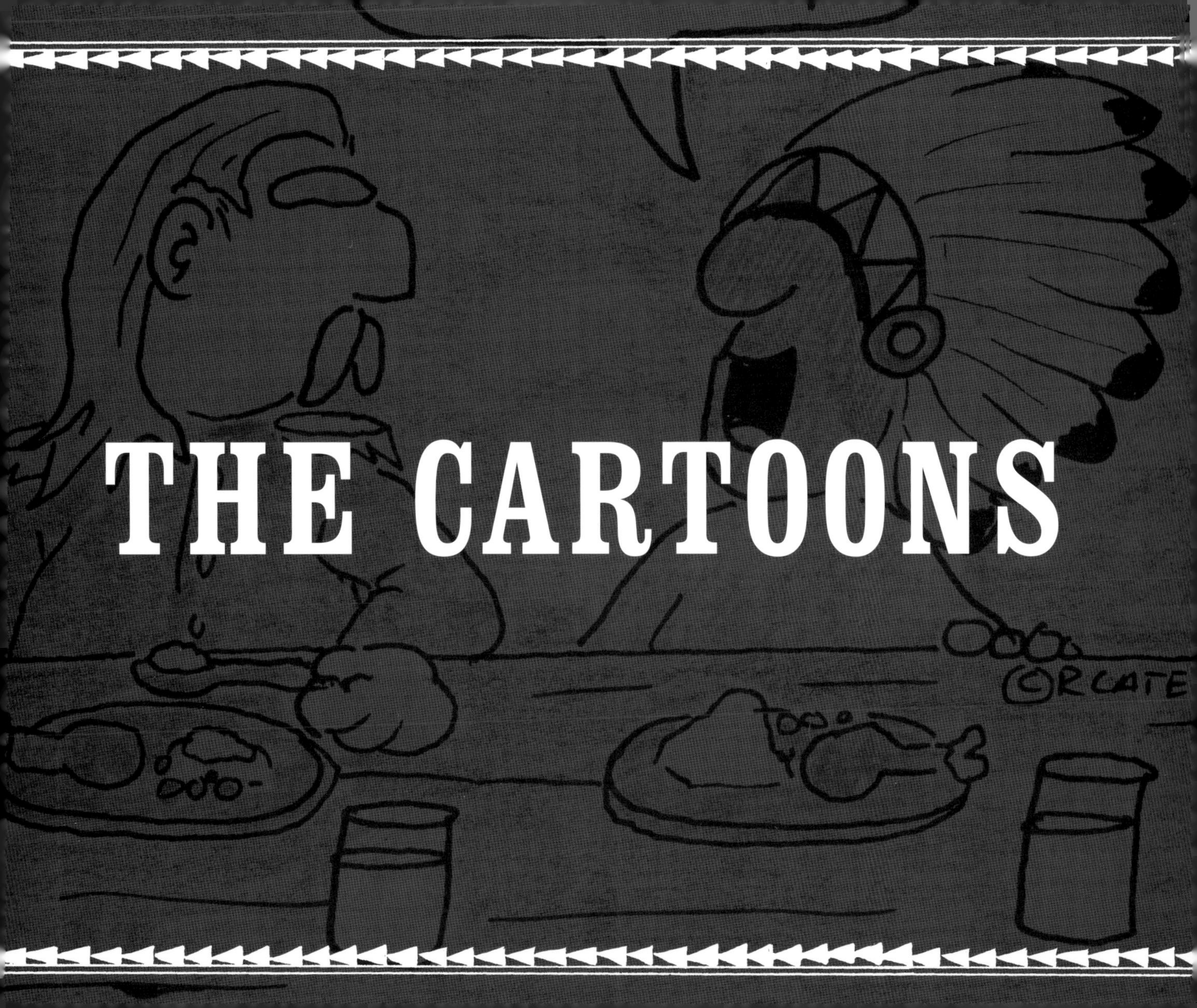
©RCATE

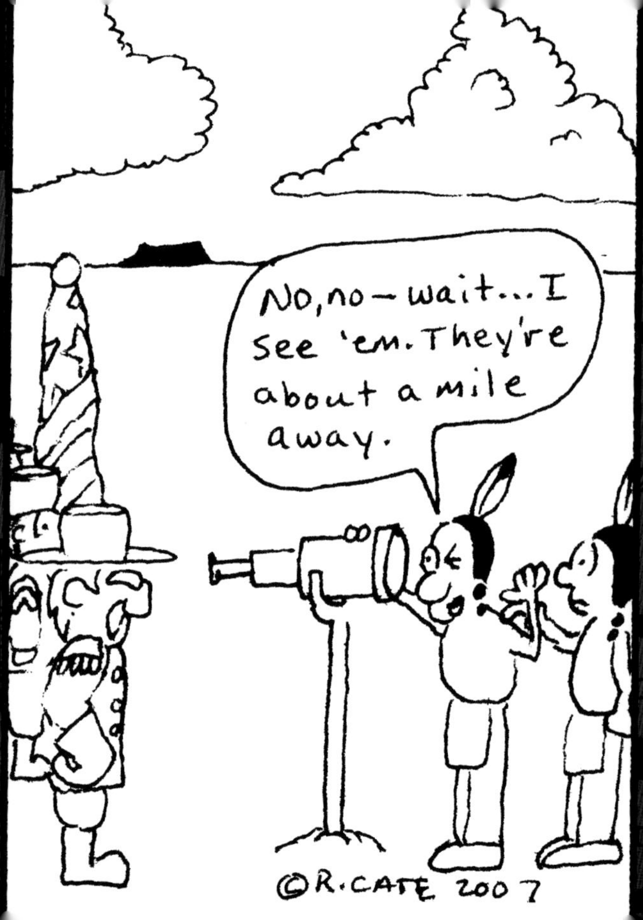
No, no – wait... I see 'em. They're about a mile away.
©R.CATE 2007

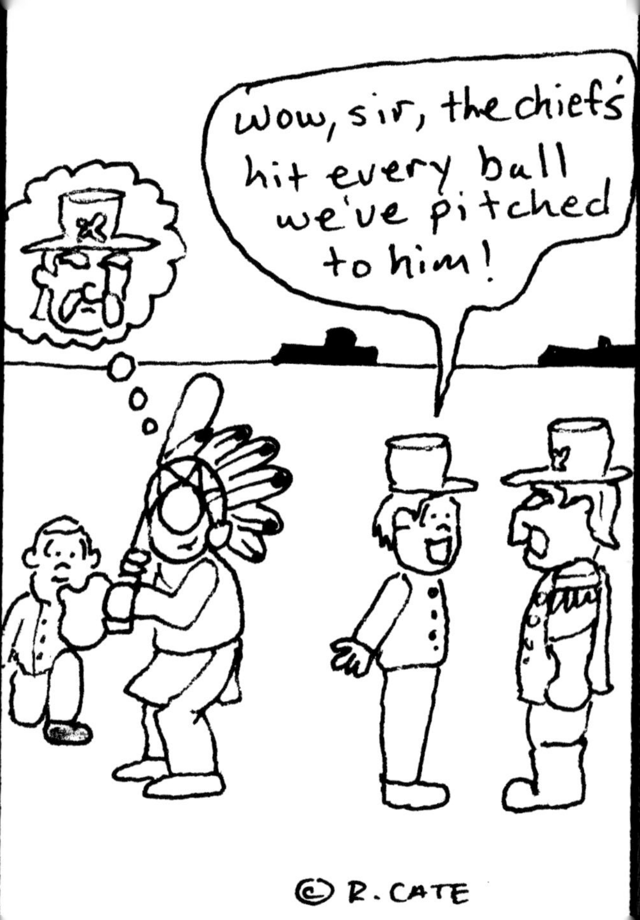
wow, sir, the chiefs' hit every ball we've pitched to him!
© R.CATE

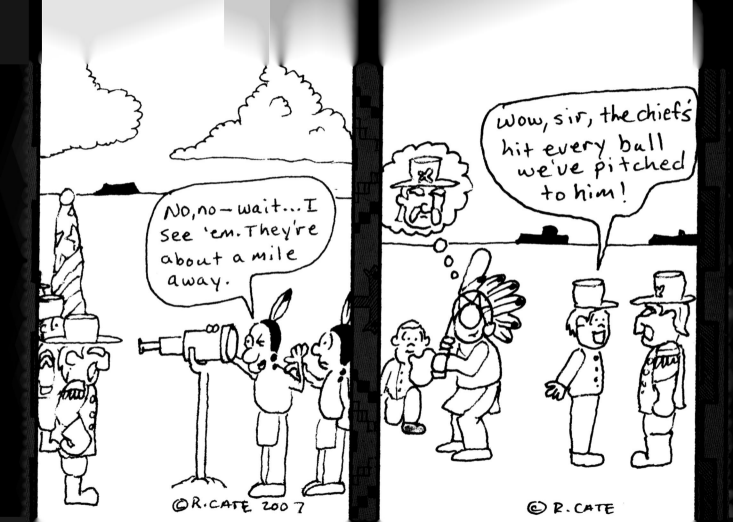

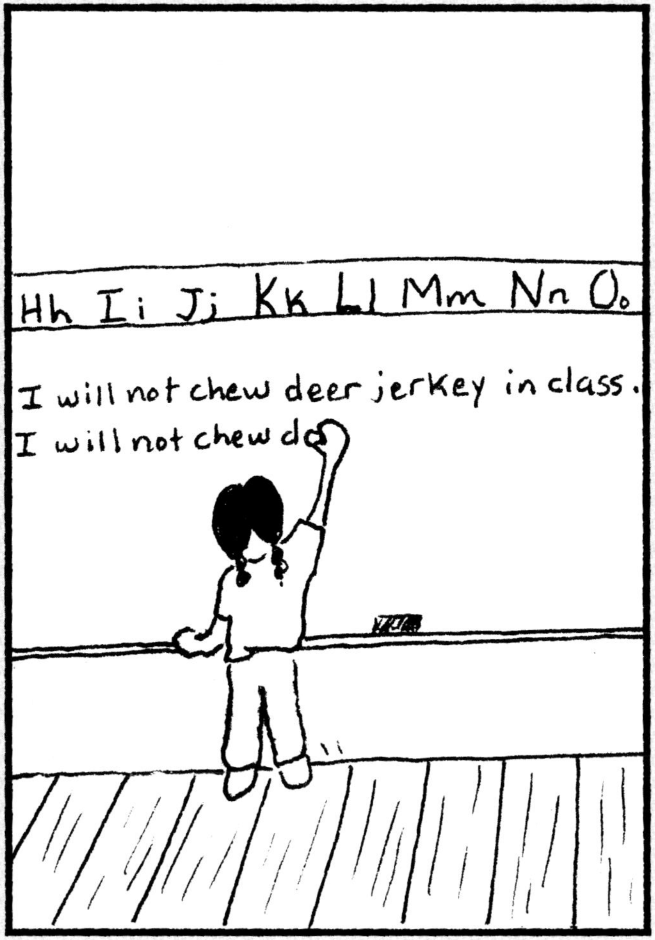
Hh Ii Jj Kk Ll Mm Nn Oo
I will not chew deer jerkey in class.
I will not chew de

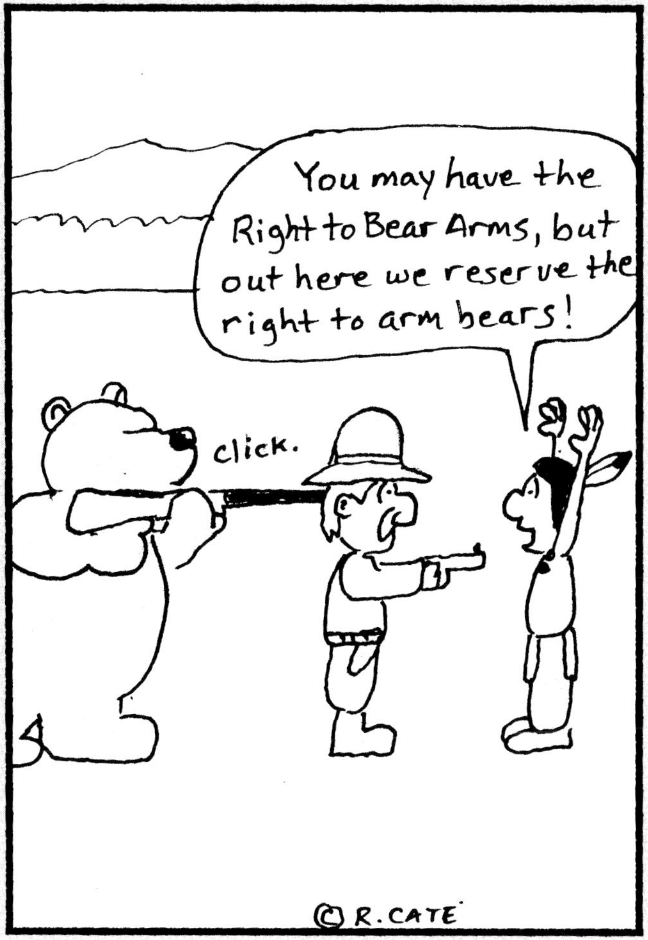
click.
You may have the Right to Bear Arms, but out here we reserve the right to arm bears!
© R. CATE

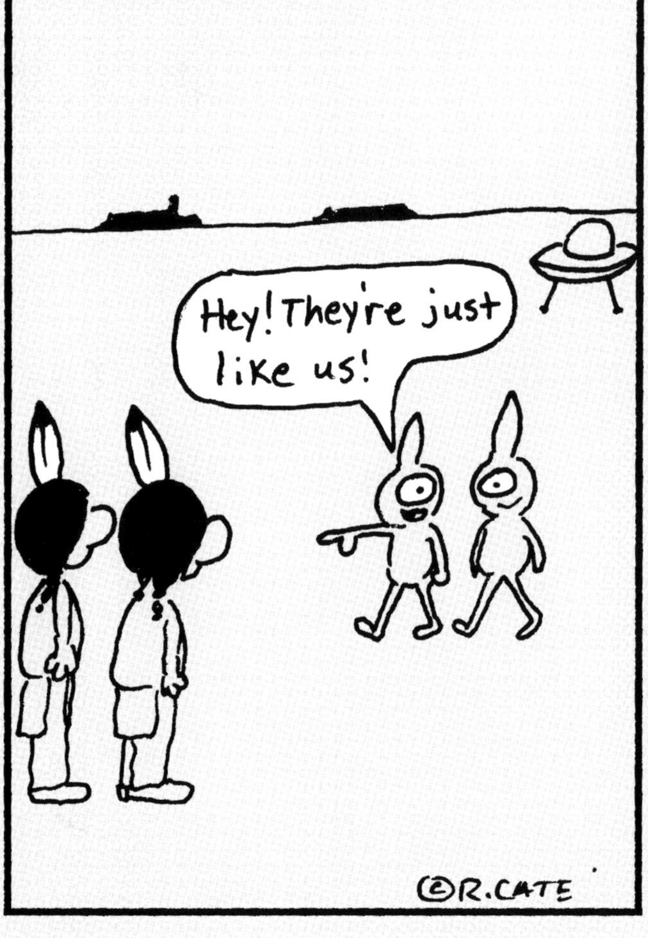
Hey! They're just like us!
©R.CATE

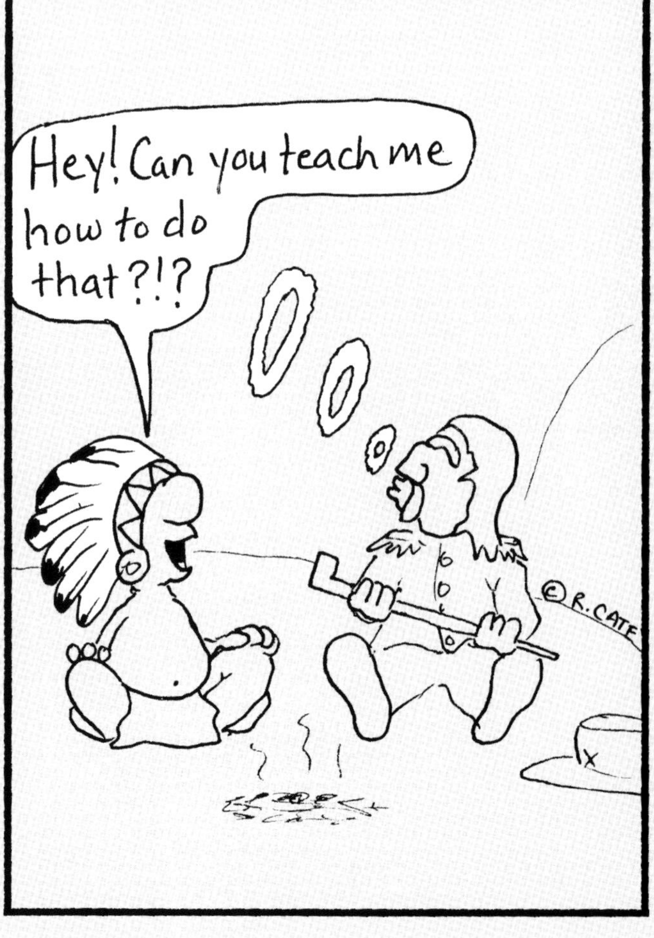
Hey! Can you teach me how to do that?!?
©R.CATE

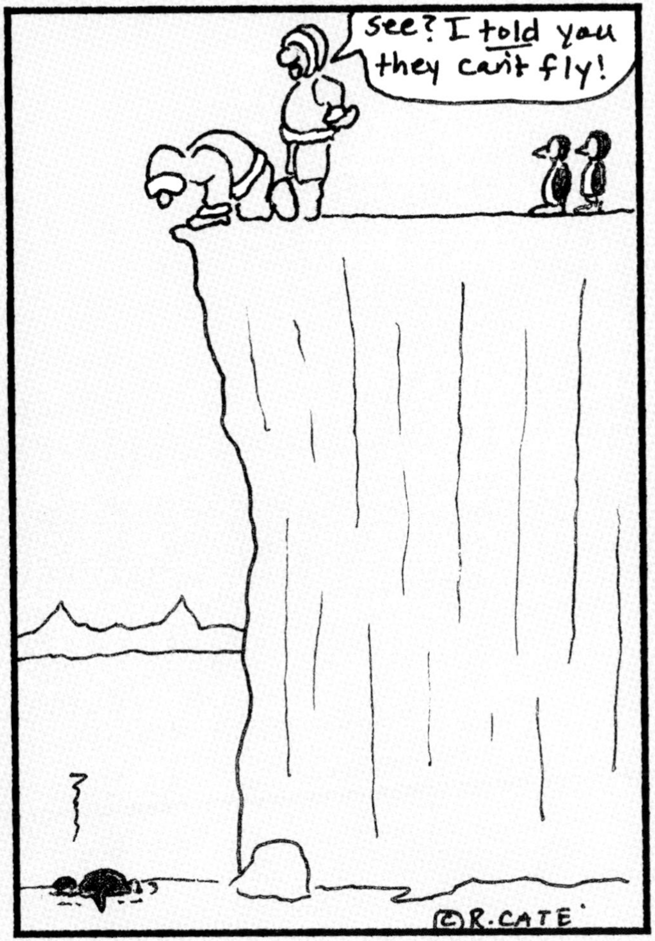
see? I told you they can't fly!
©R.CATE

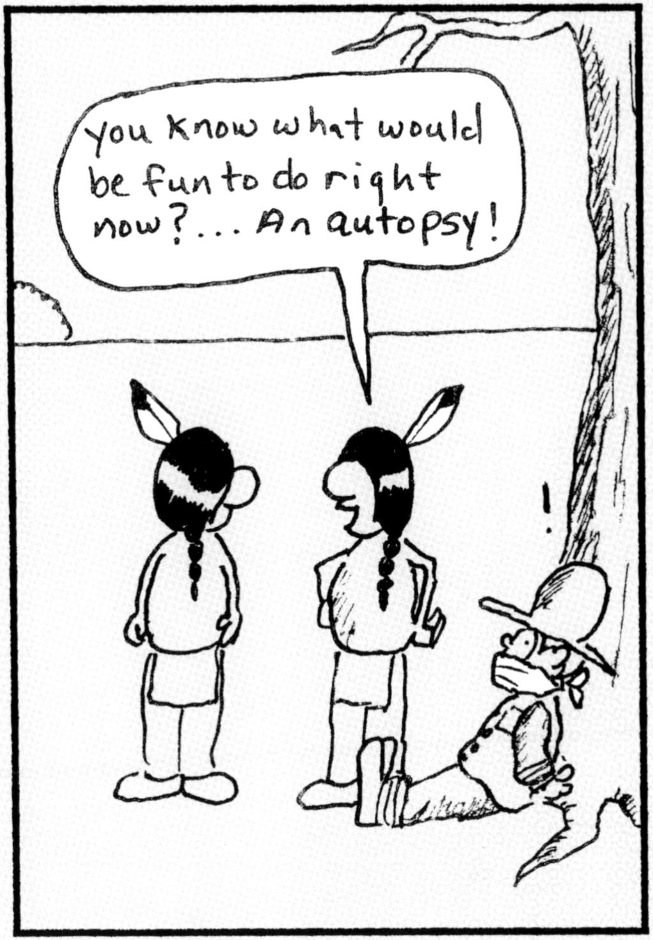
you know what would be fun to do right now?... An autopsy!
!

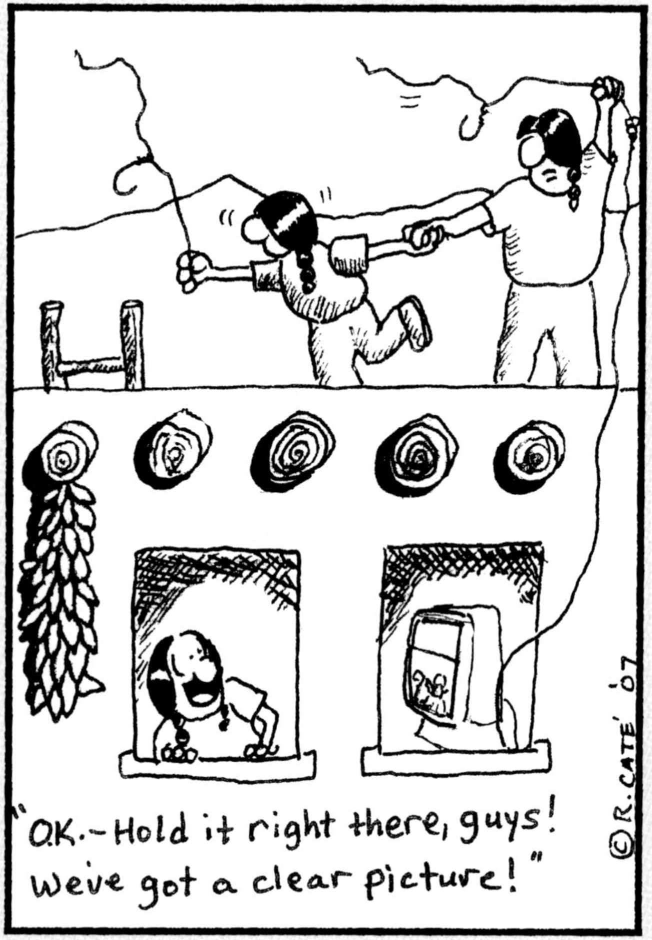
"O.K.-Hold it right there, guys! We've got a clear picture!"
©R.CATE '07

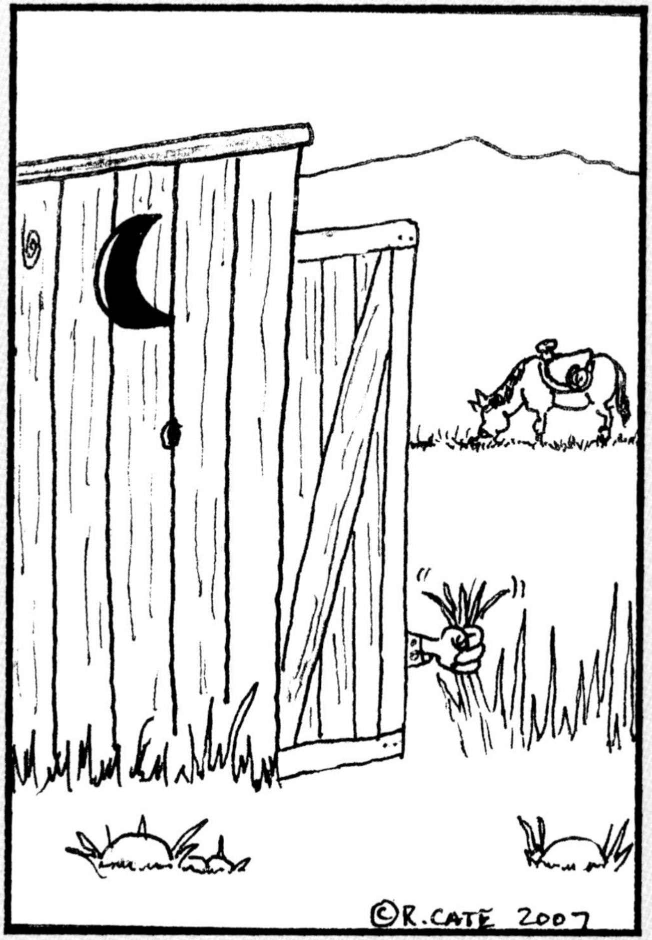
©R.CATE 2007

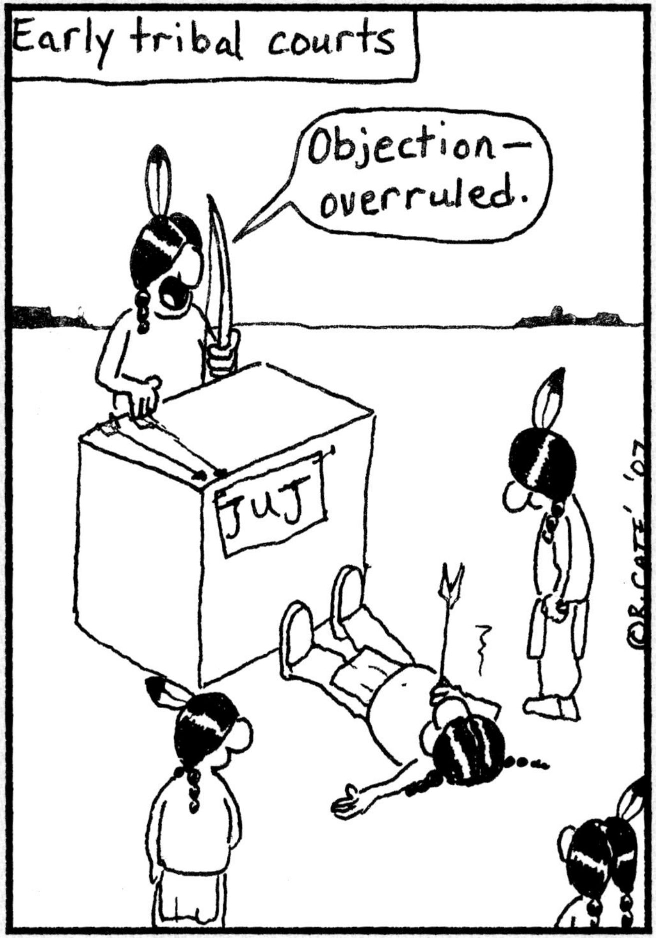
Early tribal courts
Objection— overruled.
JUJ
©R.CATE' '07

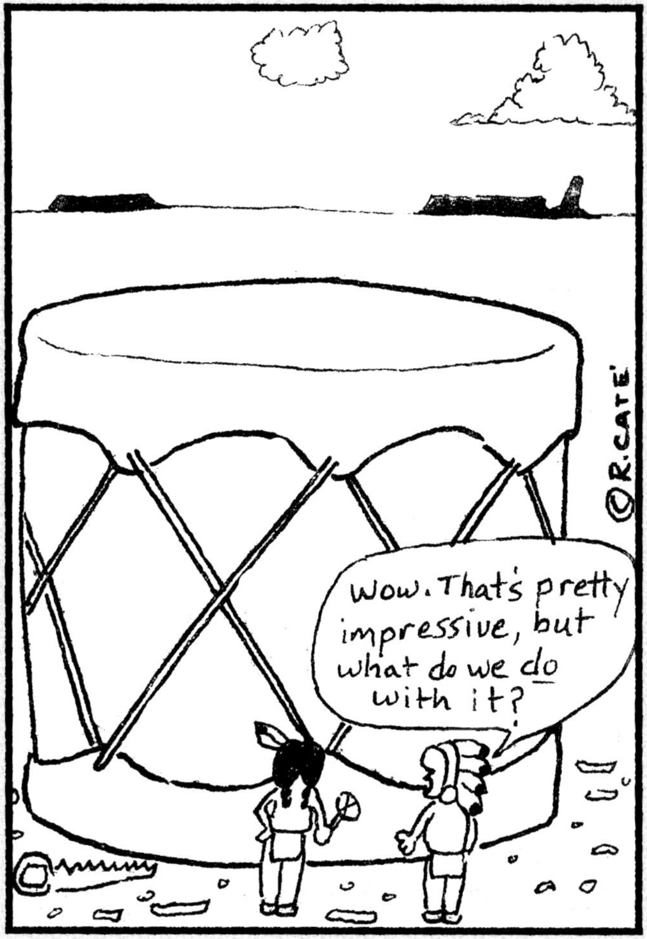
©R.CATE'
Wow. That's pretty impressive, but what do we do with it?

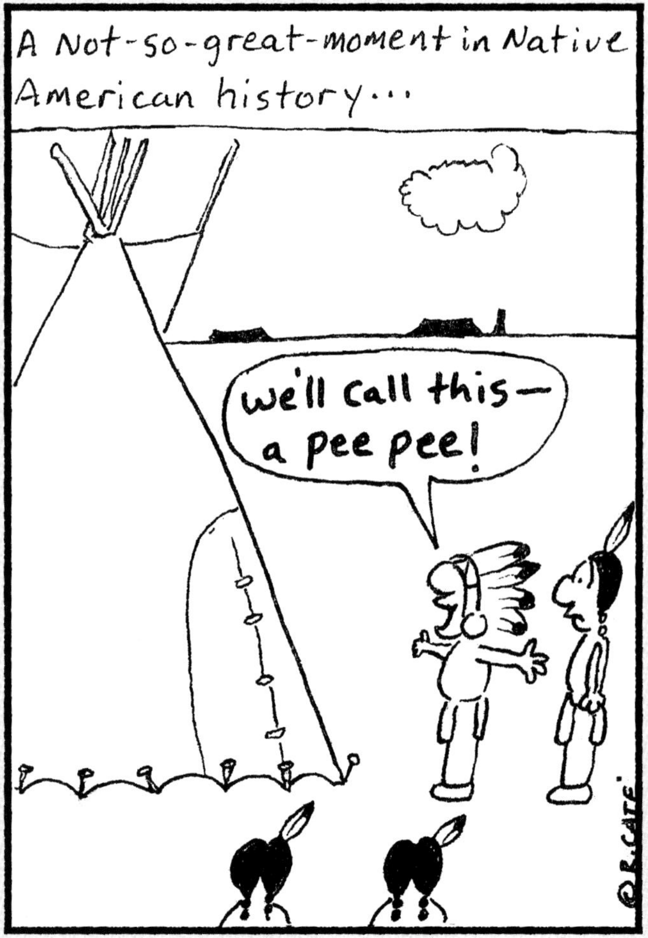
A Not-so-great-moment in Native American history...
we'll call this—a pee pee!
©R.CATE

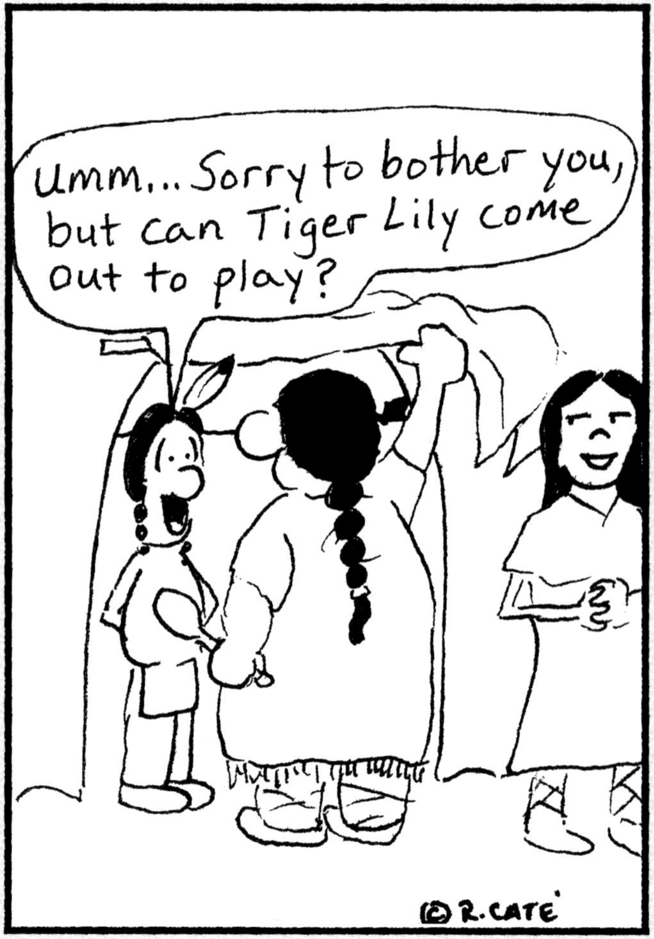
Umm... Sorry to bother you, but can Tiger Lily come out to play?
©R.CATE

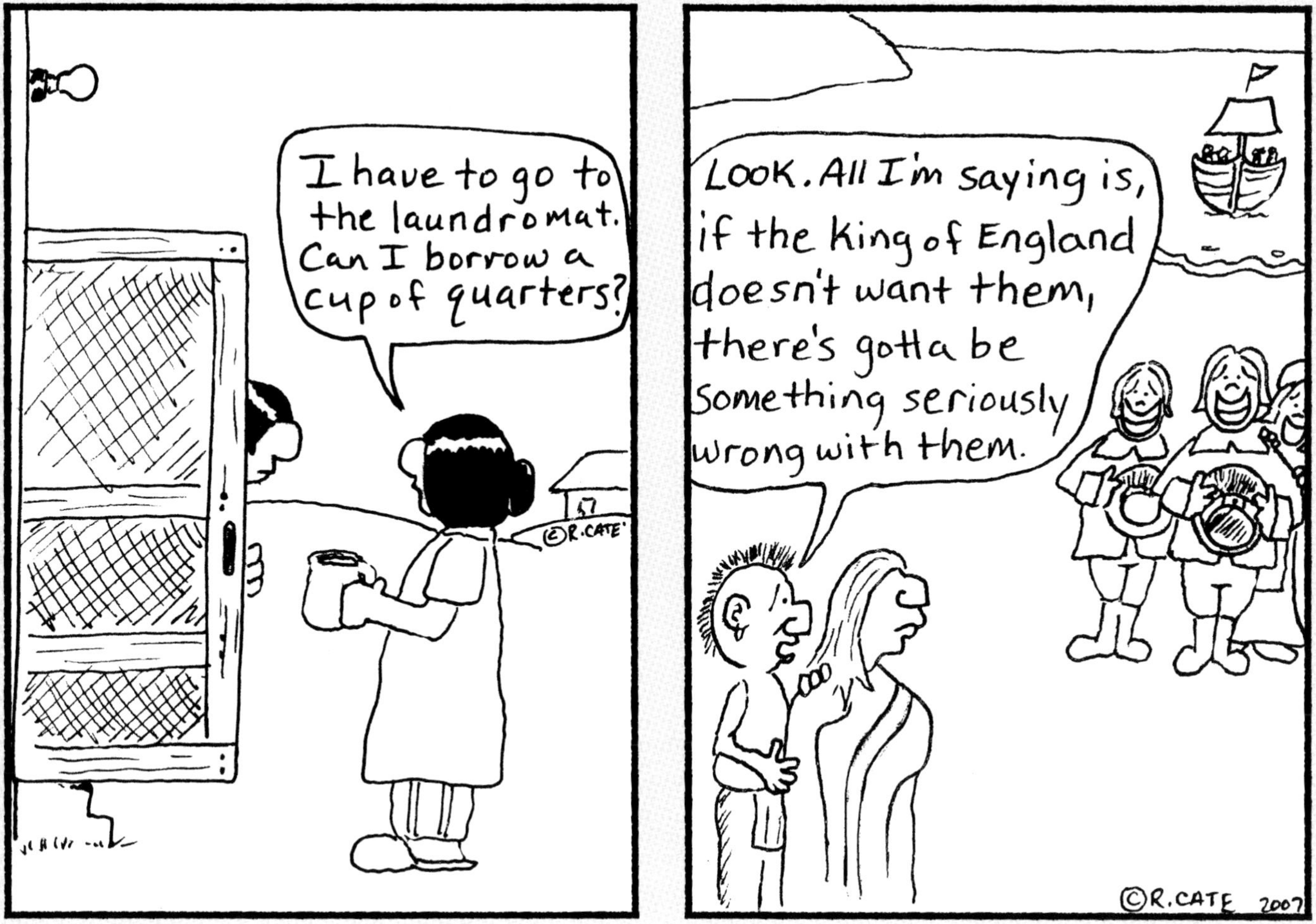
I have to go to the laundromat. Can I borrow a cup of quarters?
©R.CATE
LOOK. All I'm saying is, if the King of England doesn't want them, there's gotta be something seriously wrong with them.
©R.CATE 2007

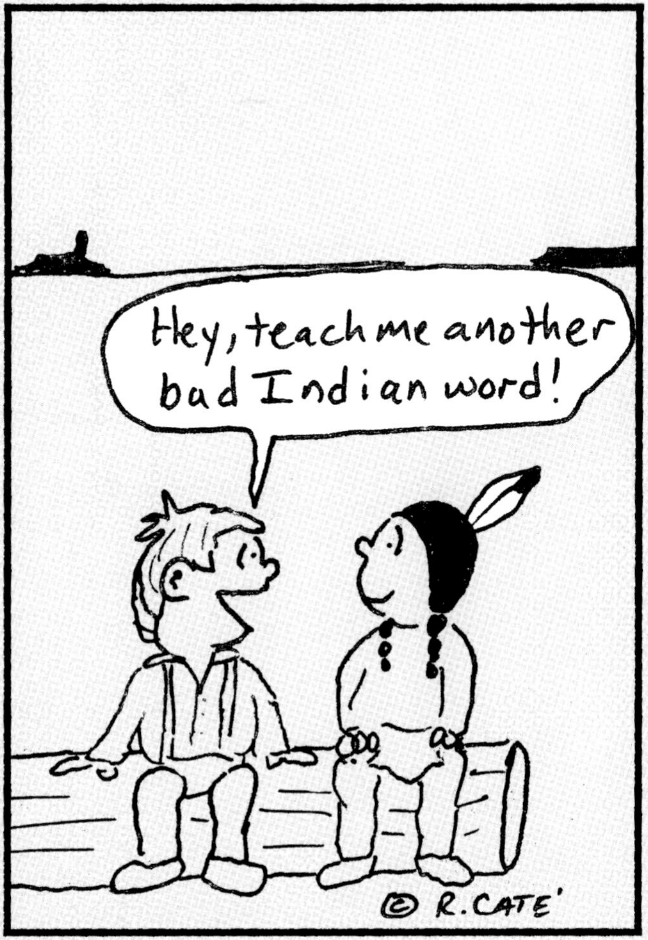
Hey, teach me another bad Indian word!
© R. CATE'

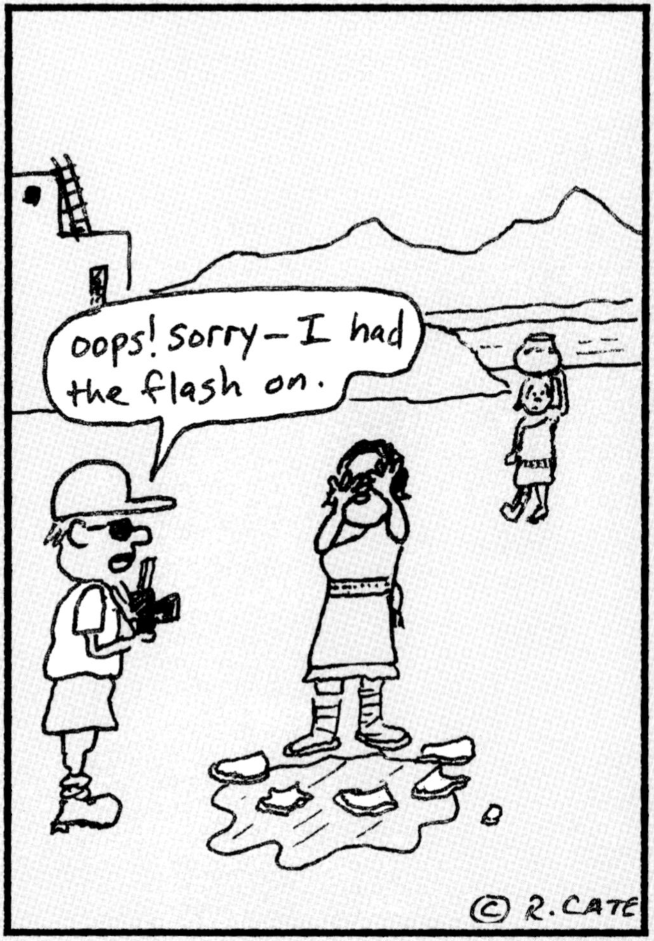
oops! sorry— I had the flash on.
© R. CATE

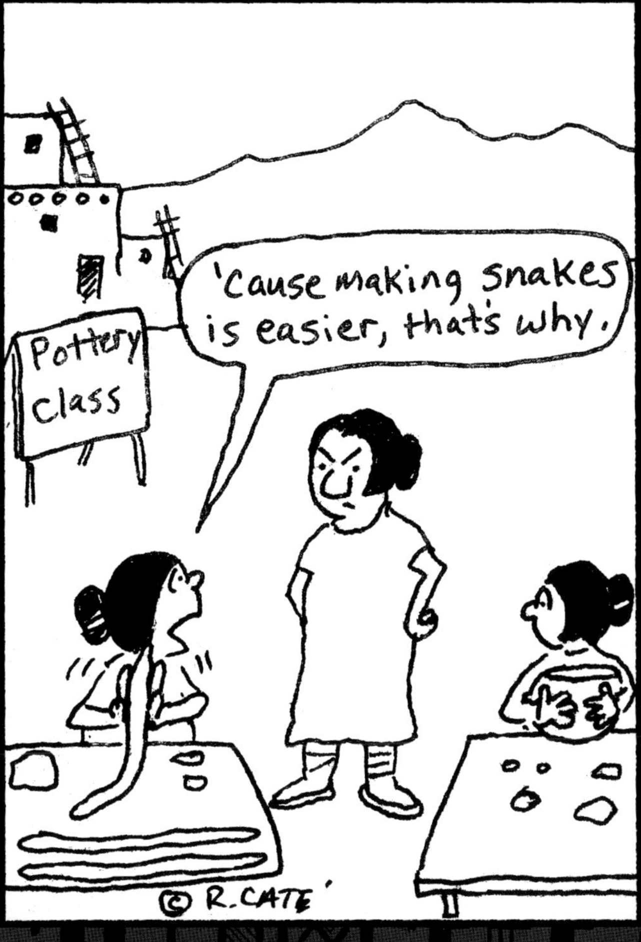
Pottery Class
'Cause making snakes is easier, that's why.
© R. CATE

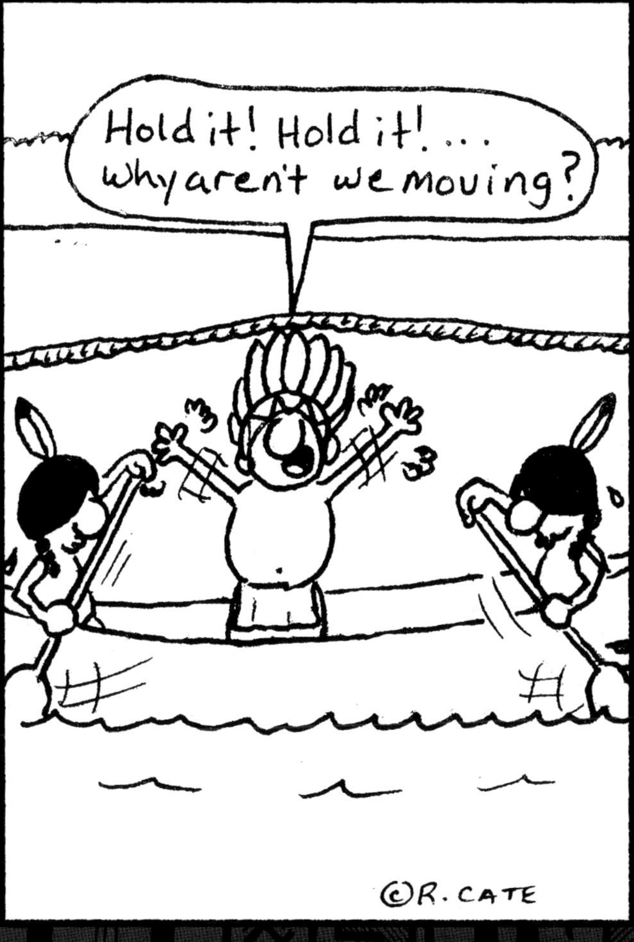
Hold it! Hold it! ... why aren't we moving?
©R. CATE

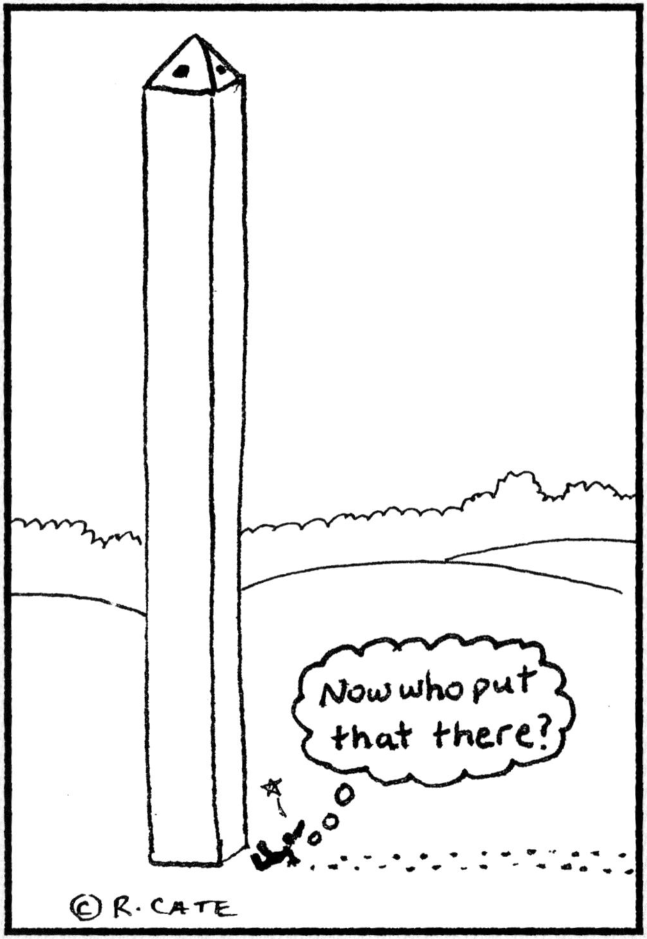
Now who put that there?
© R. CATE

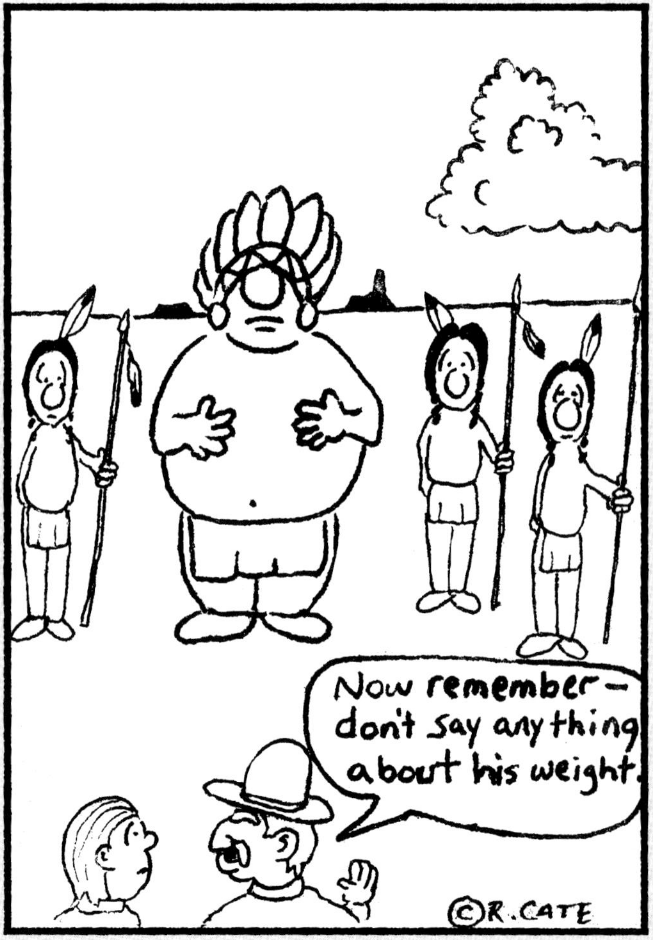
Now remember– don't say anything about his weight.
©R.CATE

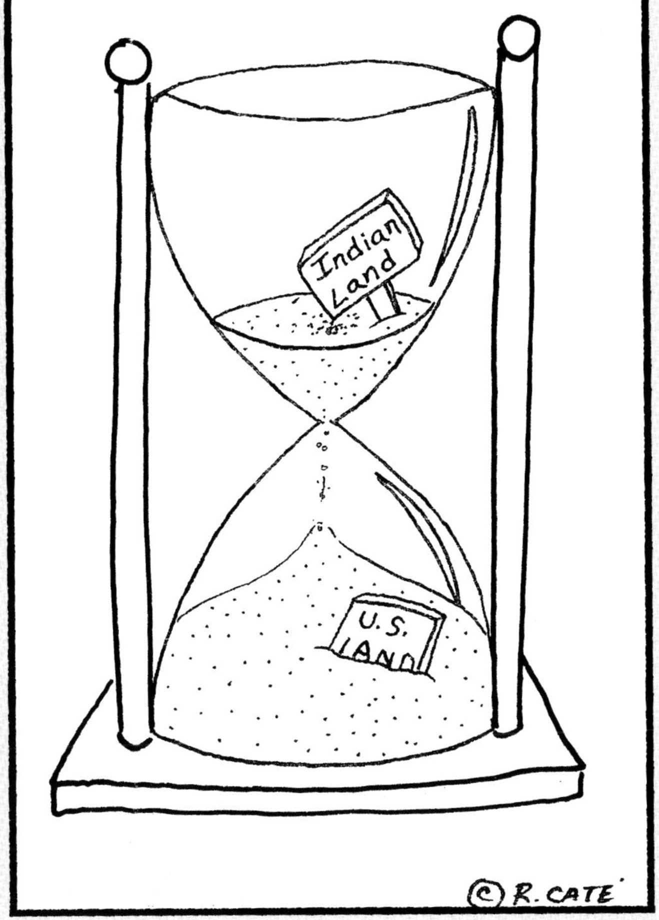
Indian Land
U.S. LAND
© R. CATE

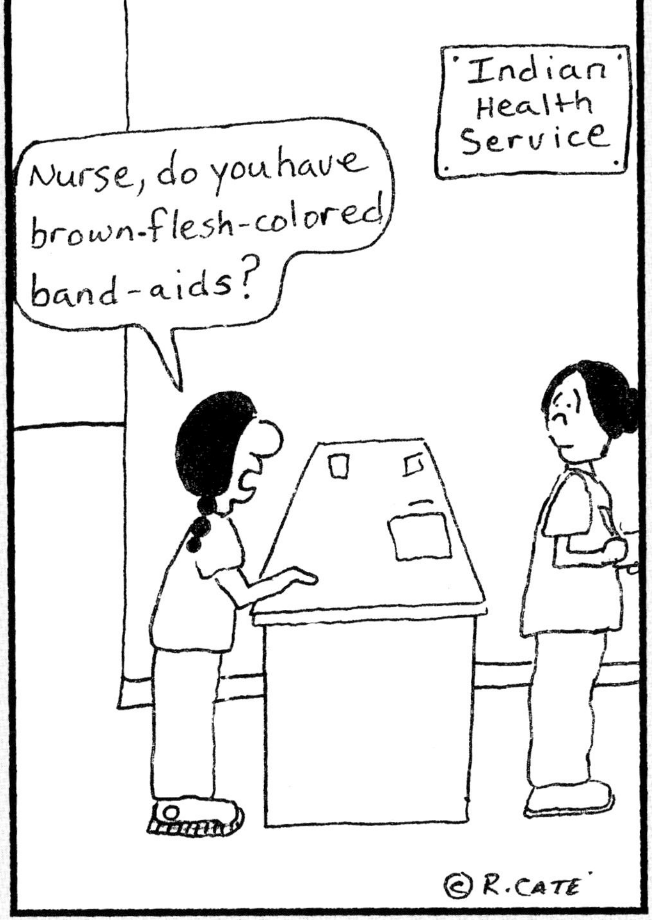
Indian Health Service
Nurse, do you have brown-flesh-colored band-aids?
© R. CATE

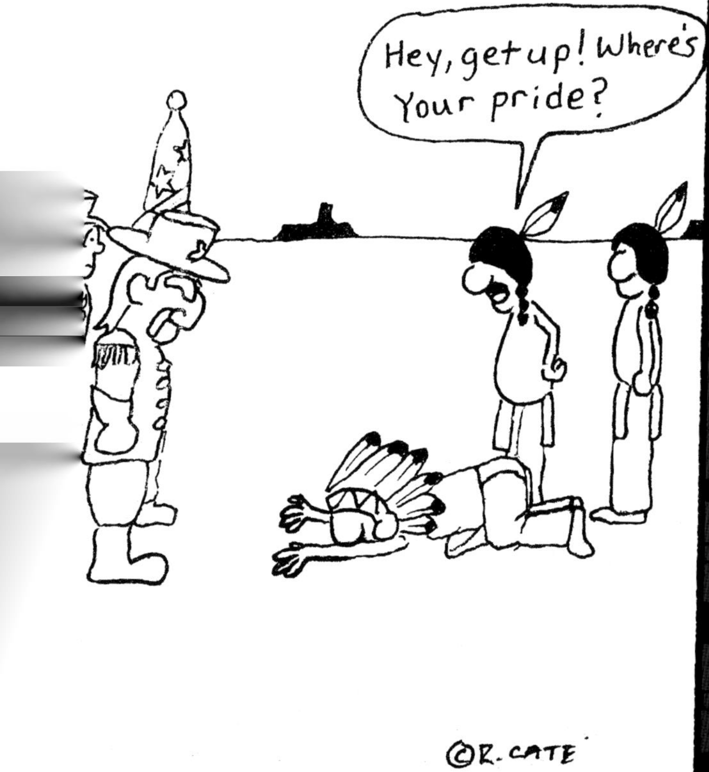
Hey, get up! Where's Your pride?
©R. CATE

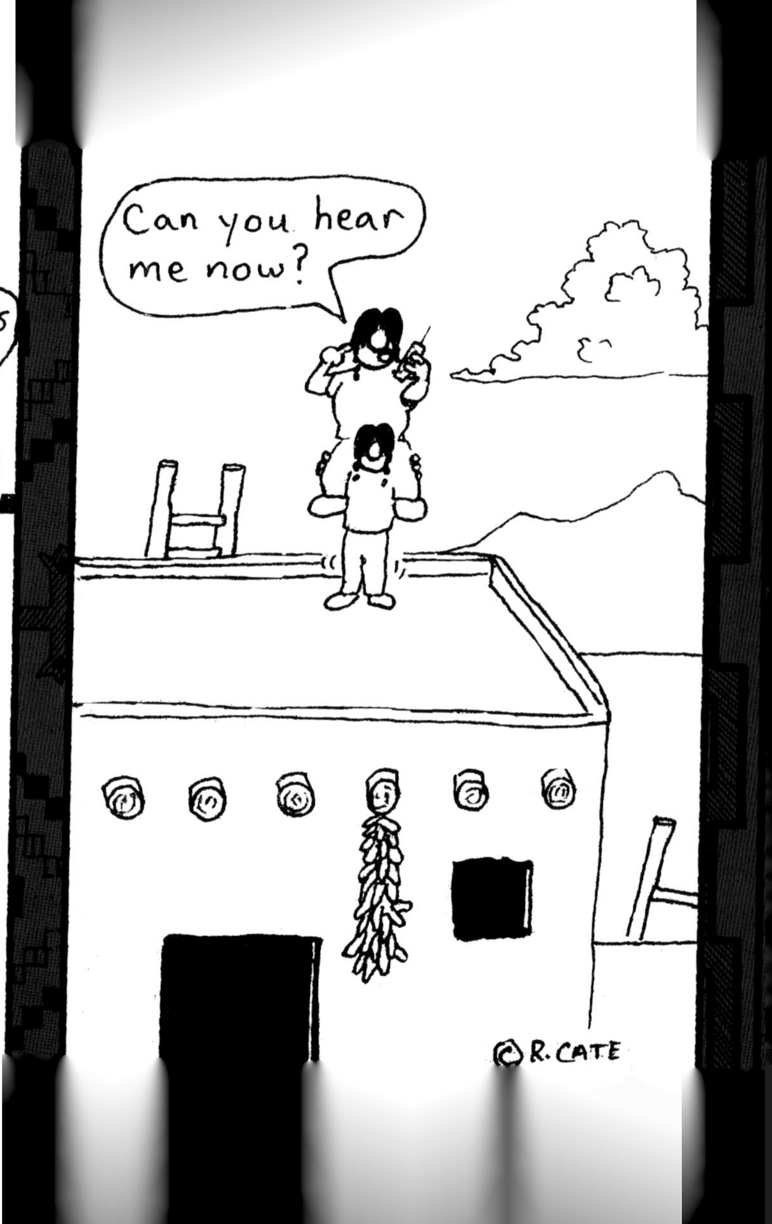
Can you hear me now?
©R. CATE

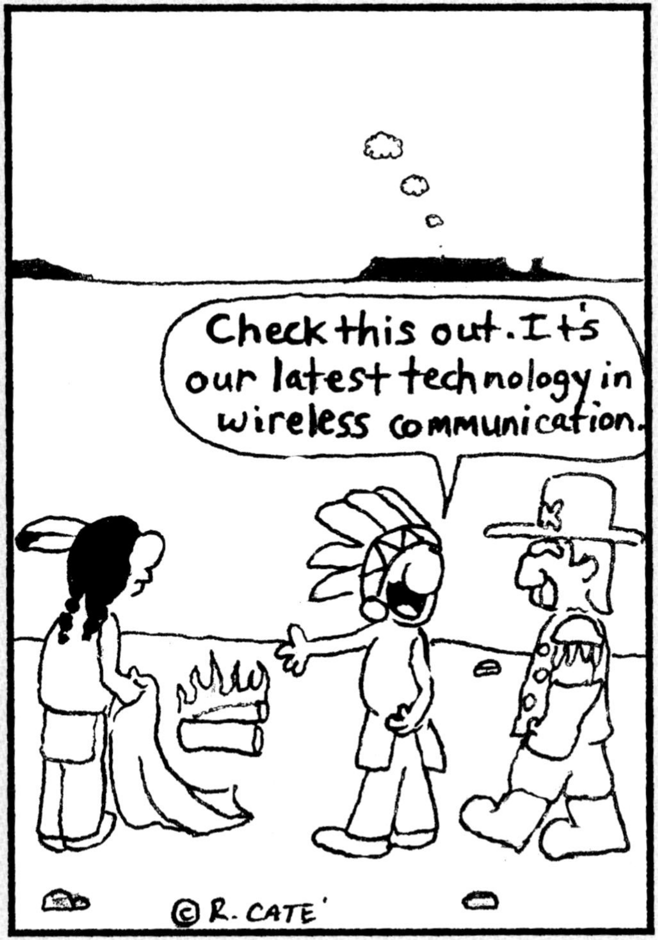
Check this out. It's our latest technology in wireless communication.
©R. CATE'

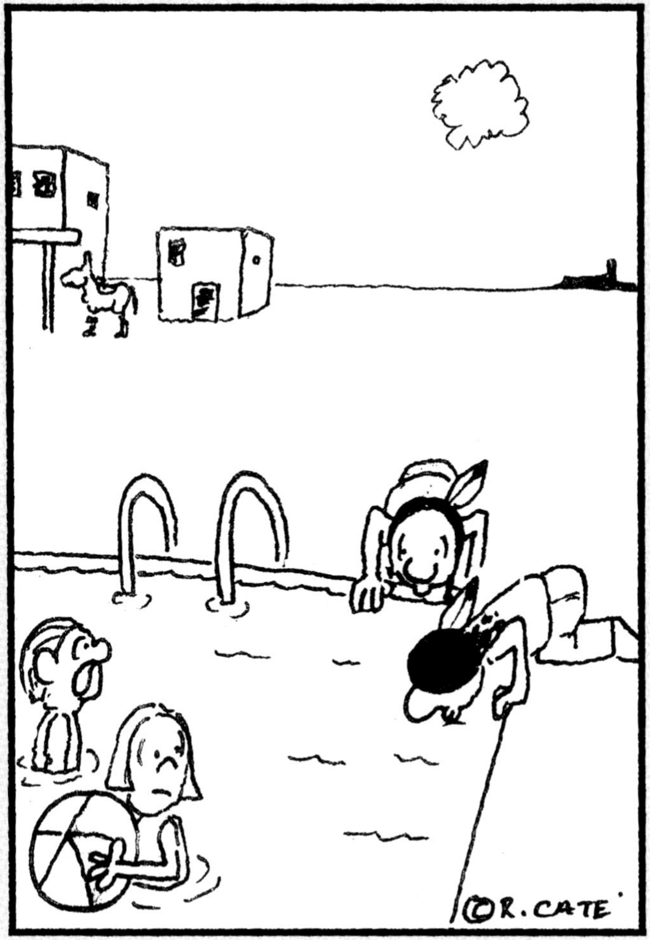
©R. CATE'

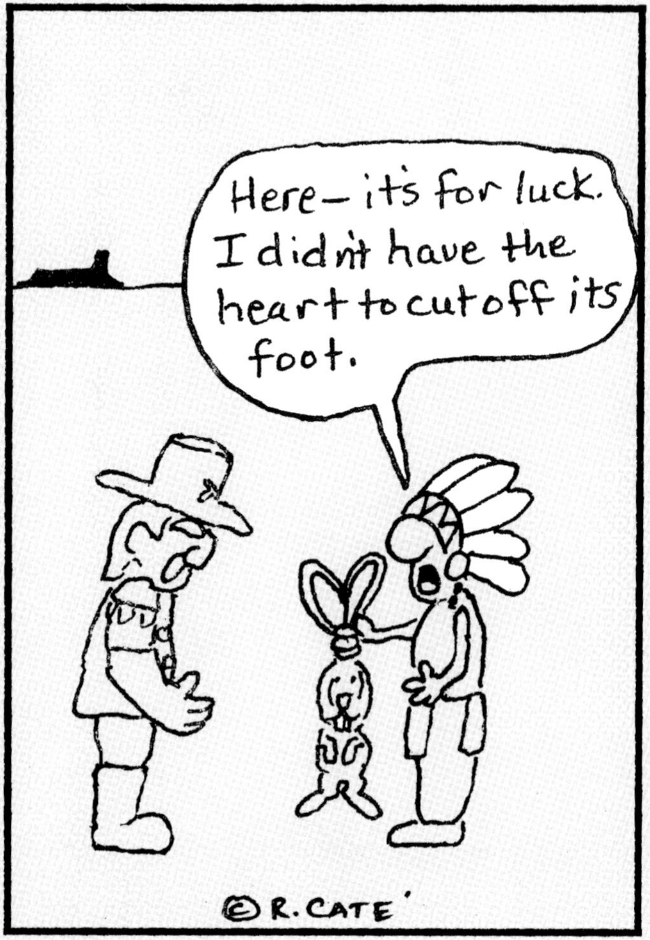
Here– it's for luck. I didn't have the heart to cut off its foot.
© R. CATE

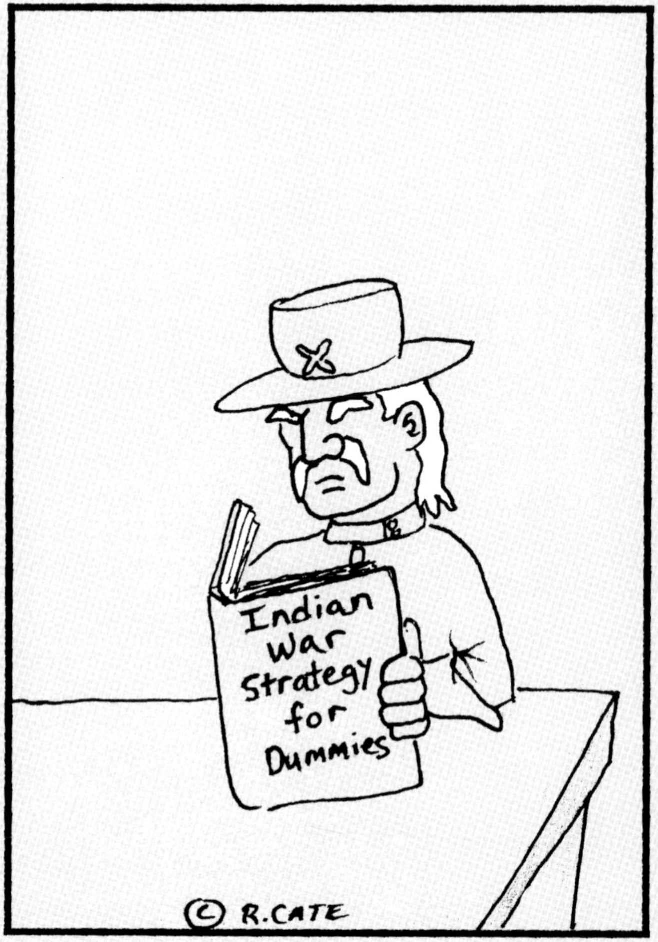
Indian War Strategy for Dummies
© R. CATE

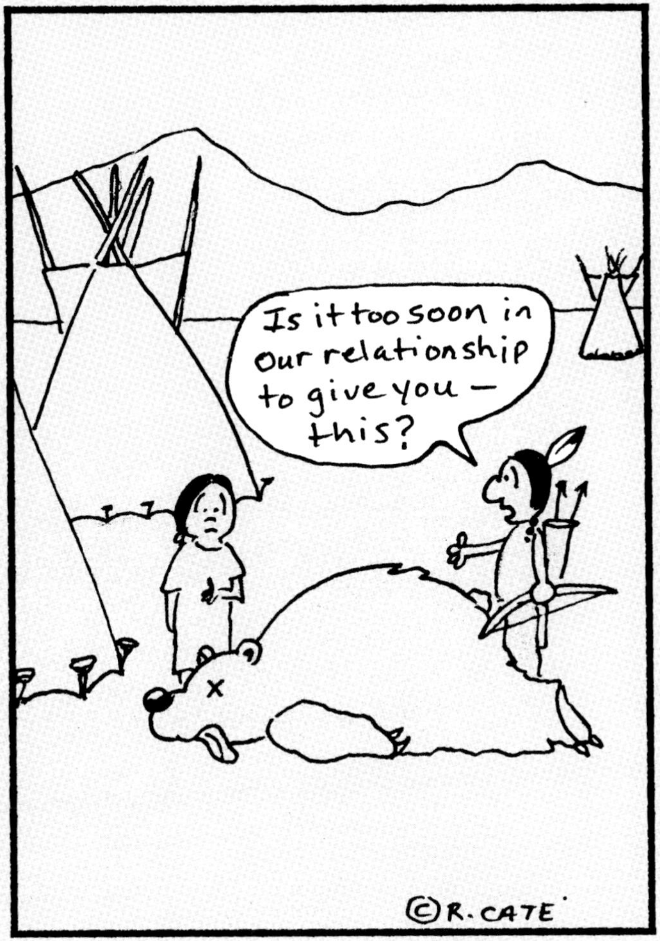
Is it too soon in our relationship to give you — this?
©R. CATE

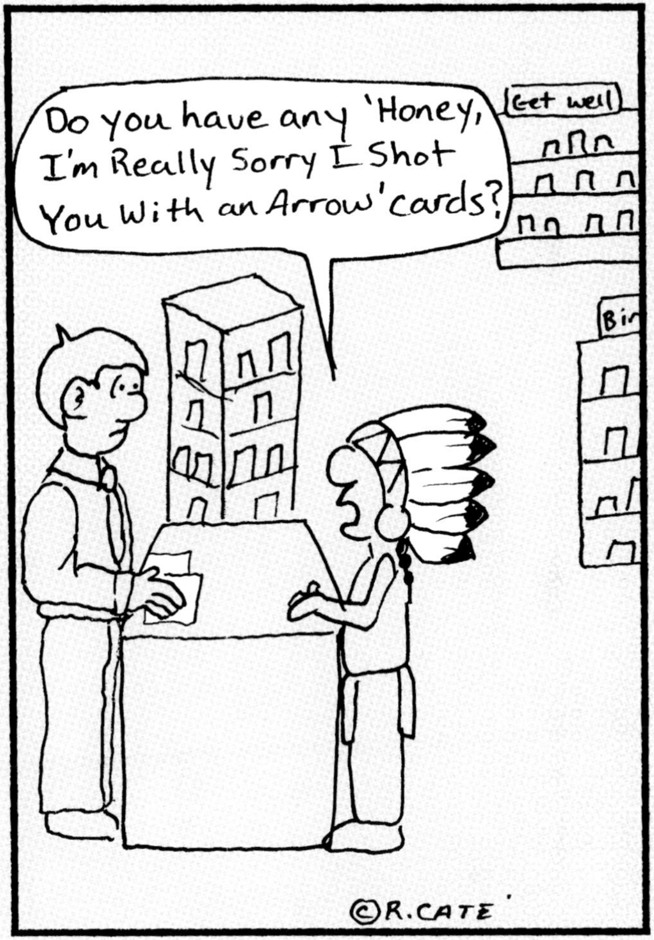
Do you have any 'Honey, I'm Really Sorry I Shot You With an Arrow' cards?
Get well
©R. CATE

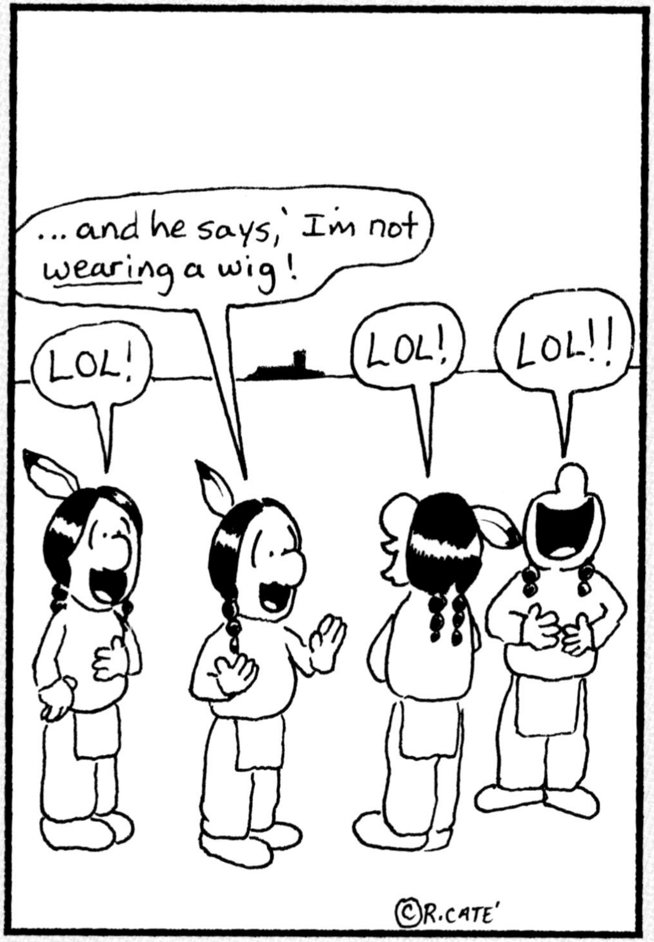
...and he says, 'I'm not wearing a wig'!
LOL!
LOL!
LOL!!
©R.CATE'

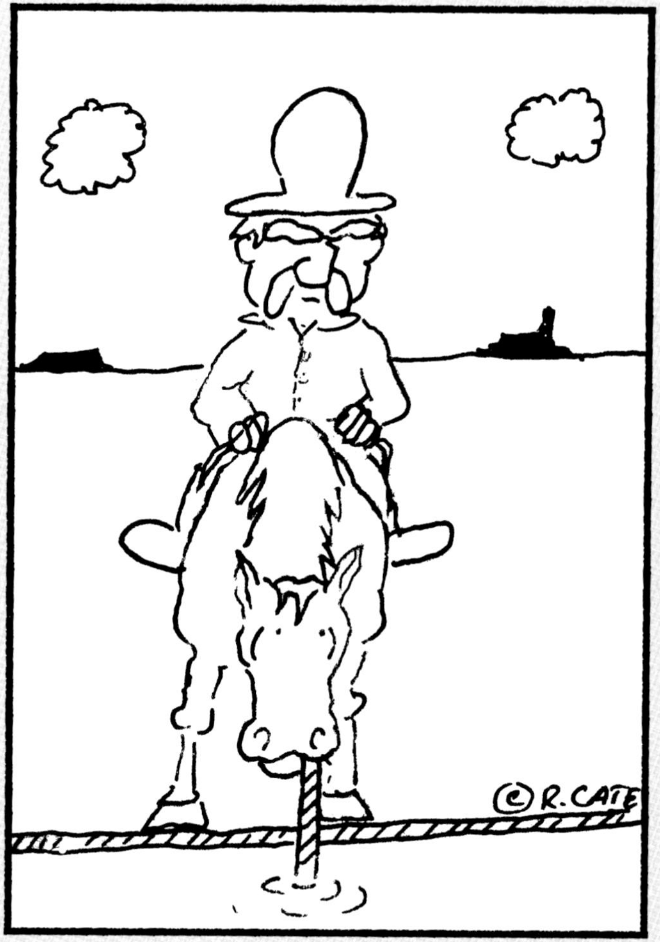
©R.CATE

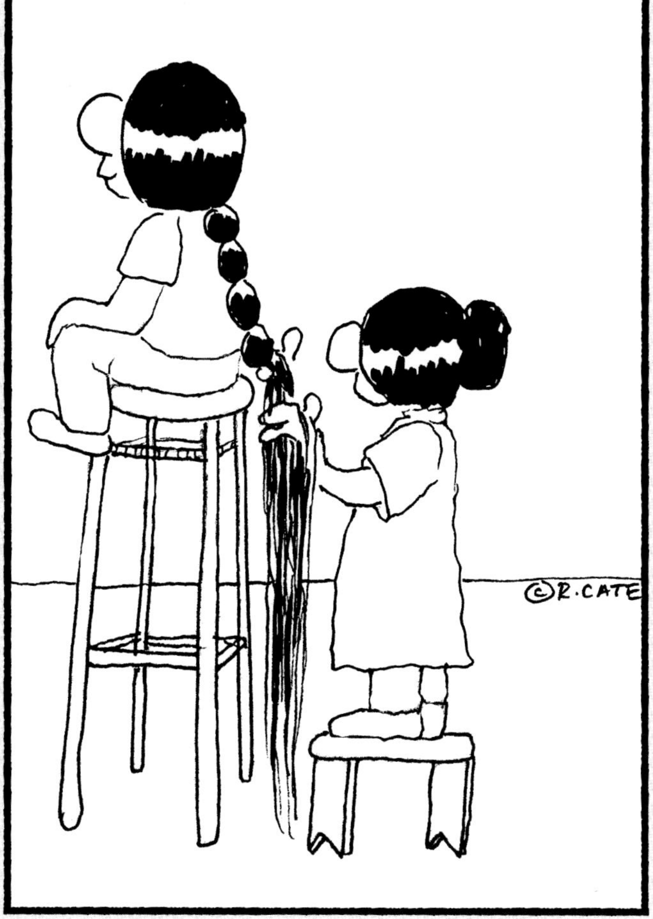
©R.CATE

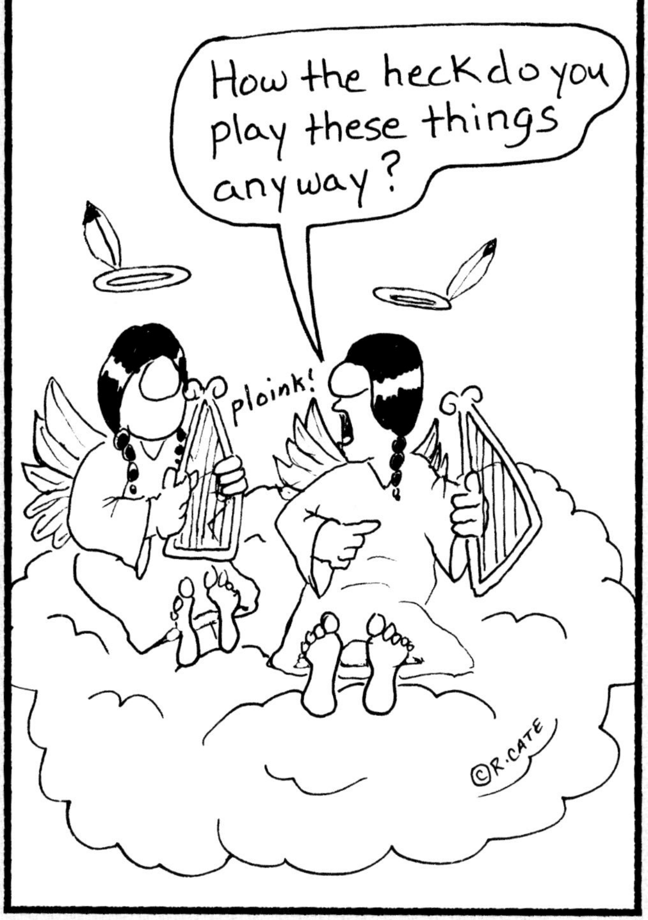
How the heck do you play these things anyway?
ploink!
©R.CATE

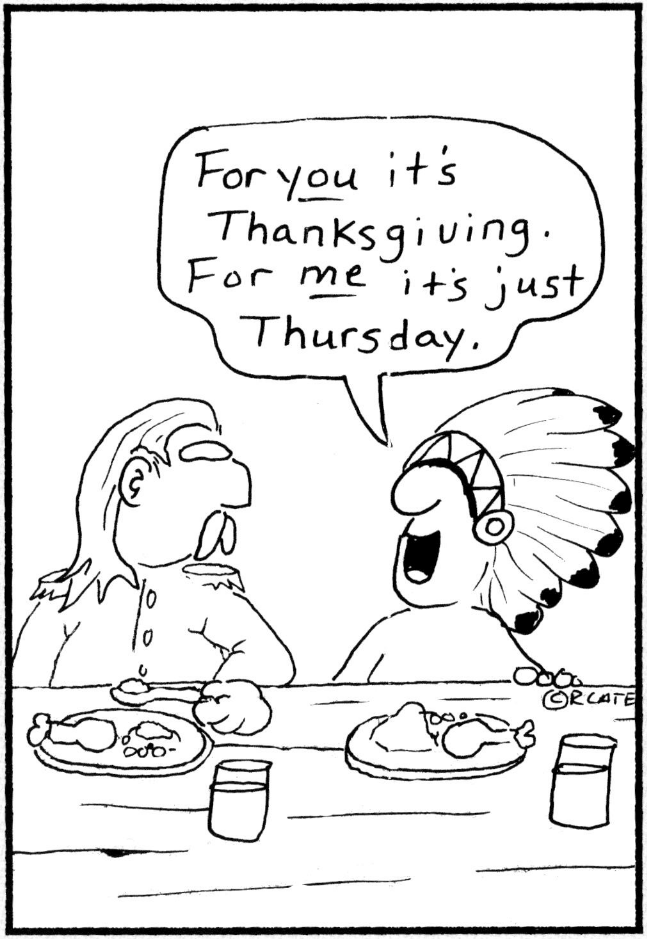
For you it's Thanksgiving. For me it's just Thursday.
©RCATE

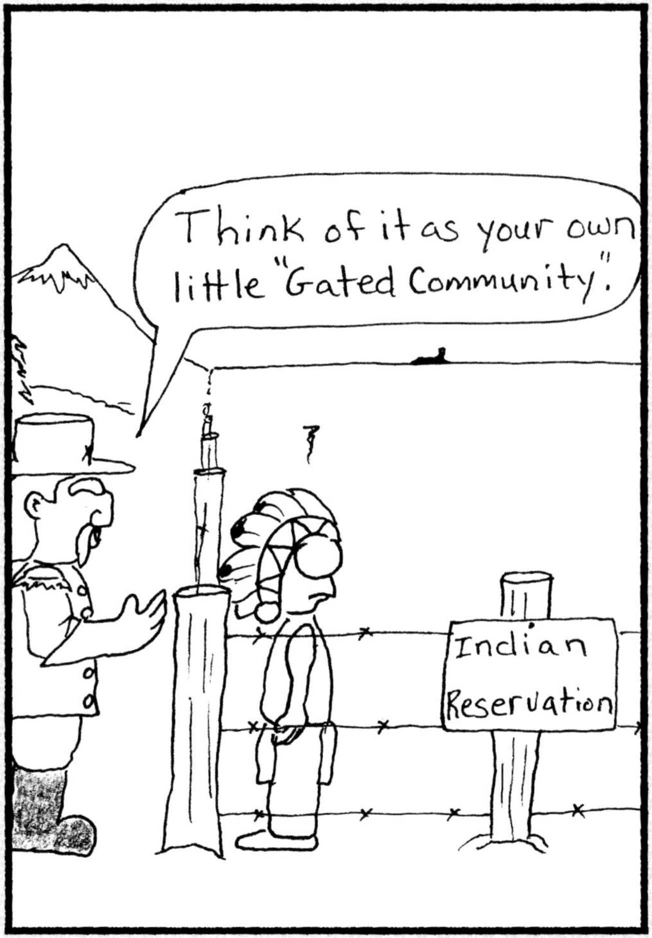
Think of it as your own little "Gated Community".
Indian Reservation

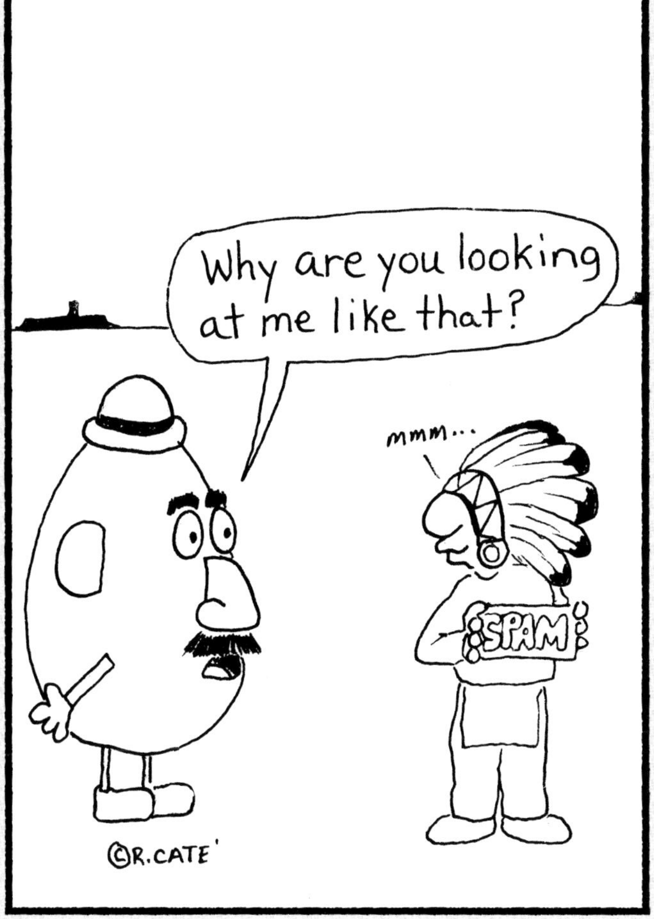
Why are you looking at me like that?
mmm...
SPAM
©R.CATE

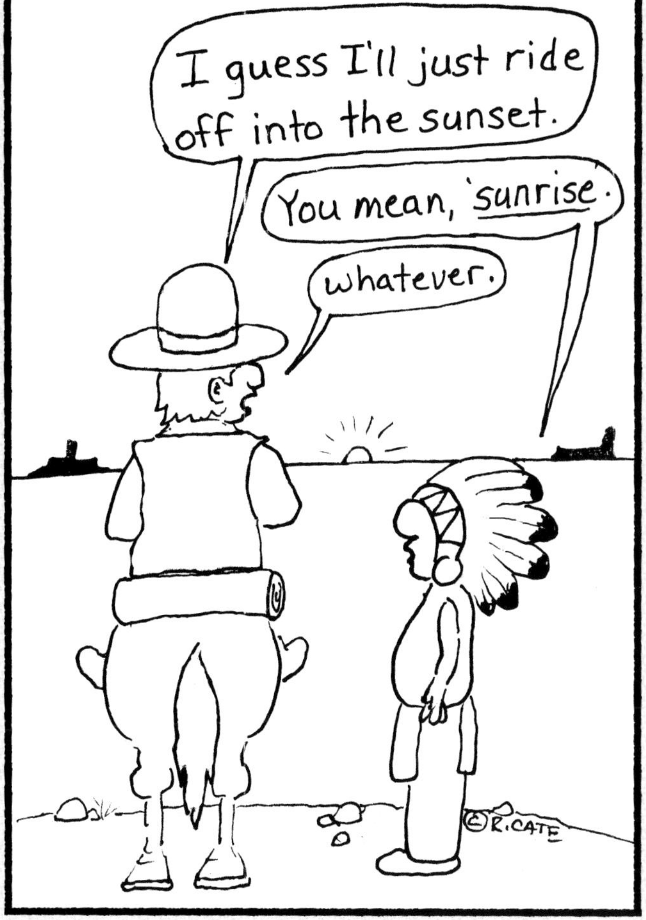
I guess I'll just ride off into the sunset.
You mean, 'sunrise'.
whatever.
©R.CATE

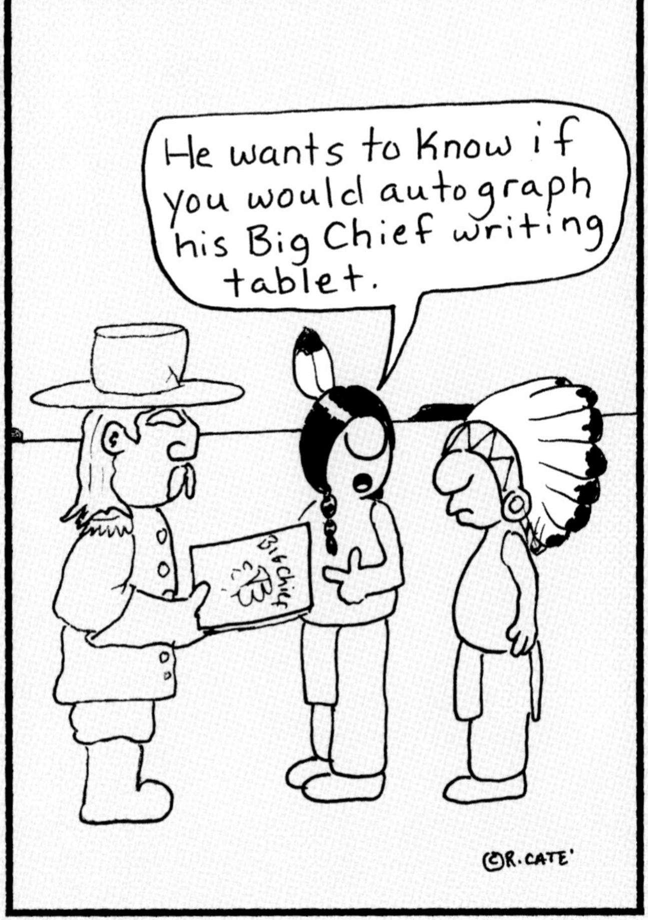
He wants to Know if you would autograph his Big Chief writing tablet.
Big Chief
©R. CATE'

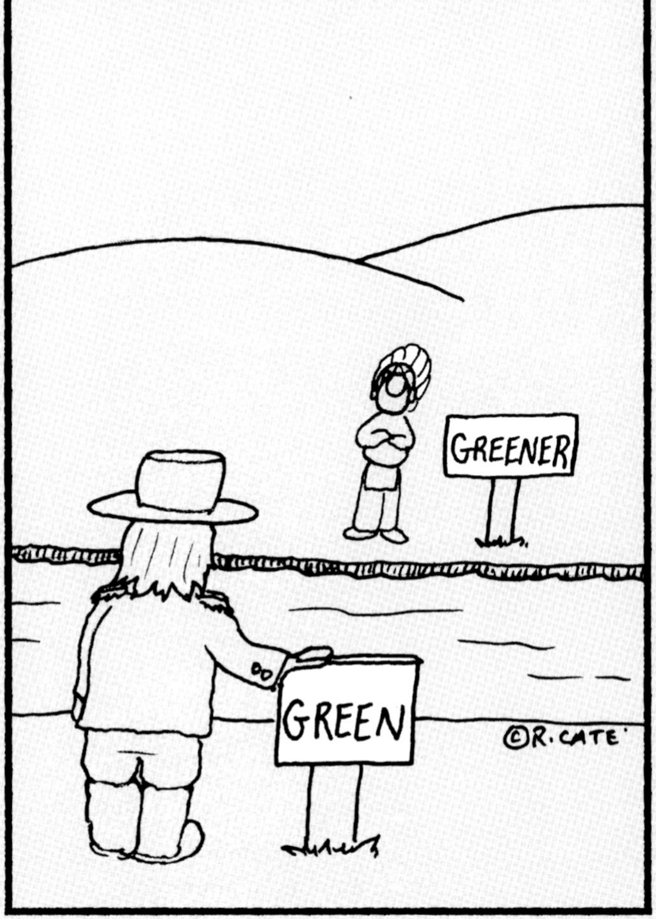
GREENER
GREEN
©R. CATE'

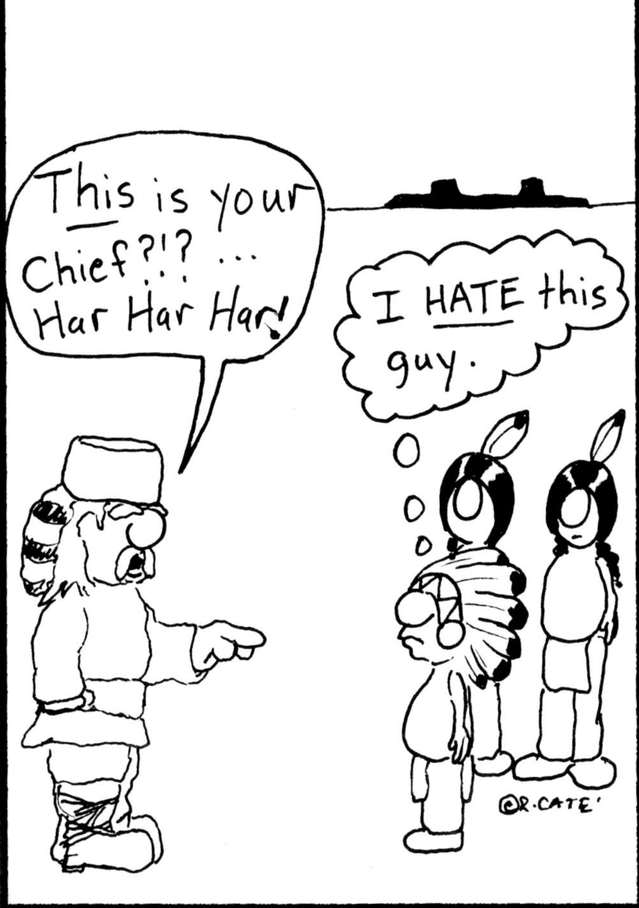
This is your Chief?!? ... Har Har Har!
I HATE this guy.
©R. CATE'

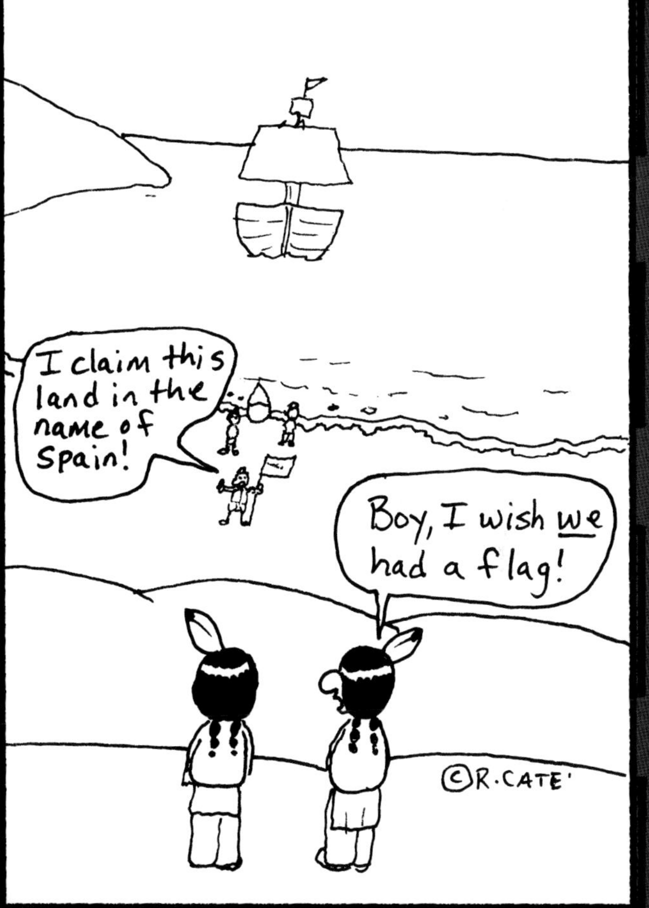
I claim this land in the name of Spain!
Boy, I wish we had a flag!
©R. CATE'

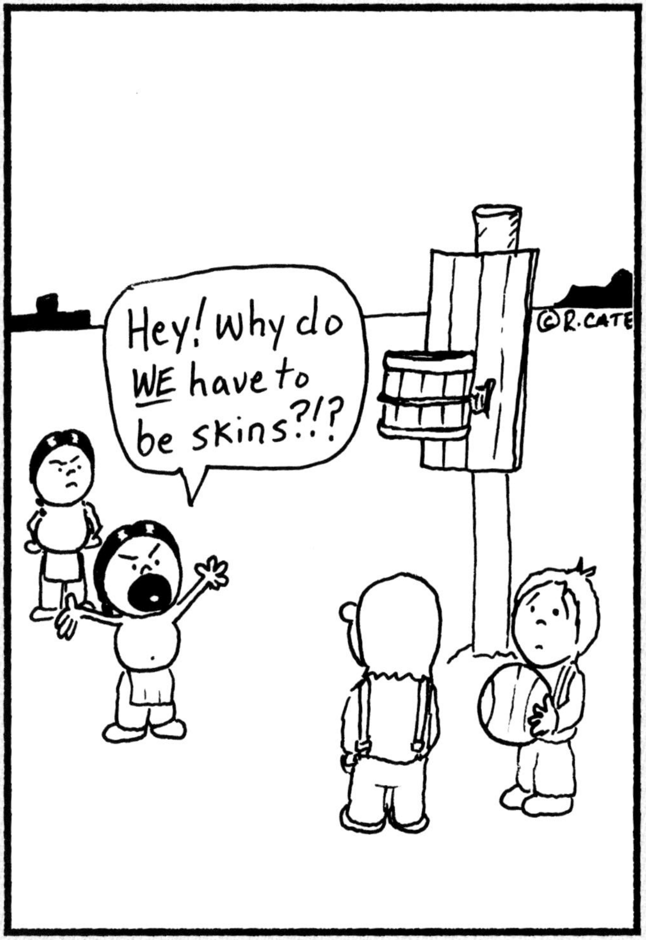
Hey! Why do WE have to be skins?!?
©R.CATE

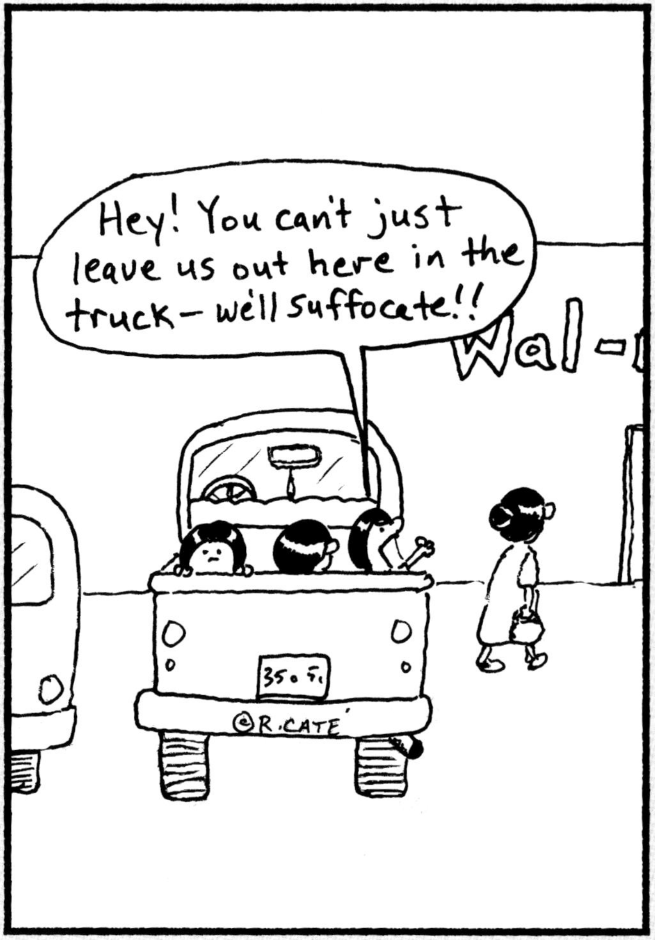
Hey! You can't just leave us out here in the truck – we'll suffocate!!
Wal-
©R.CATE

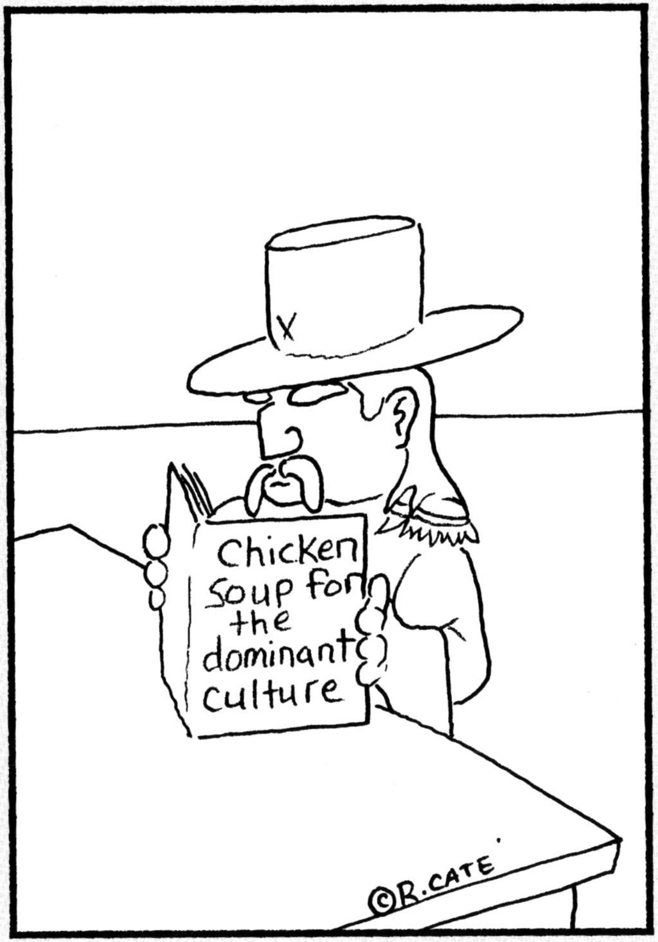
Chicken soup for the dominant culture
©R.CATE

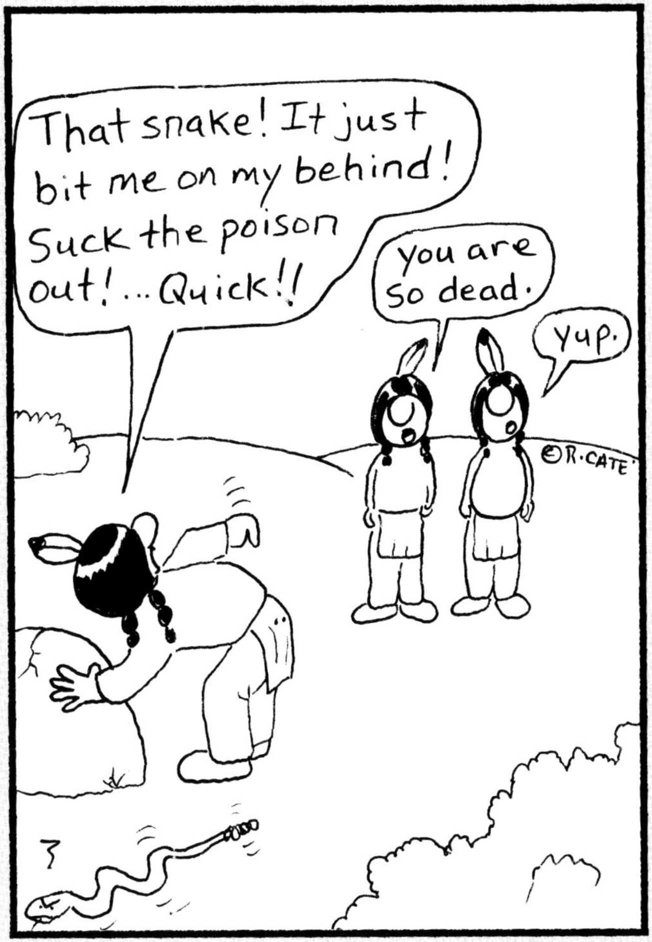
That snake! It just bit me on my behind! Suck the poison out! ... Quick!!
you are so dead.
Yup.
©R.CATE

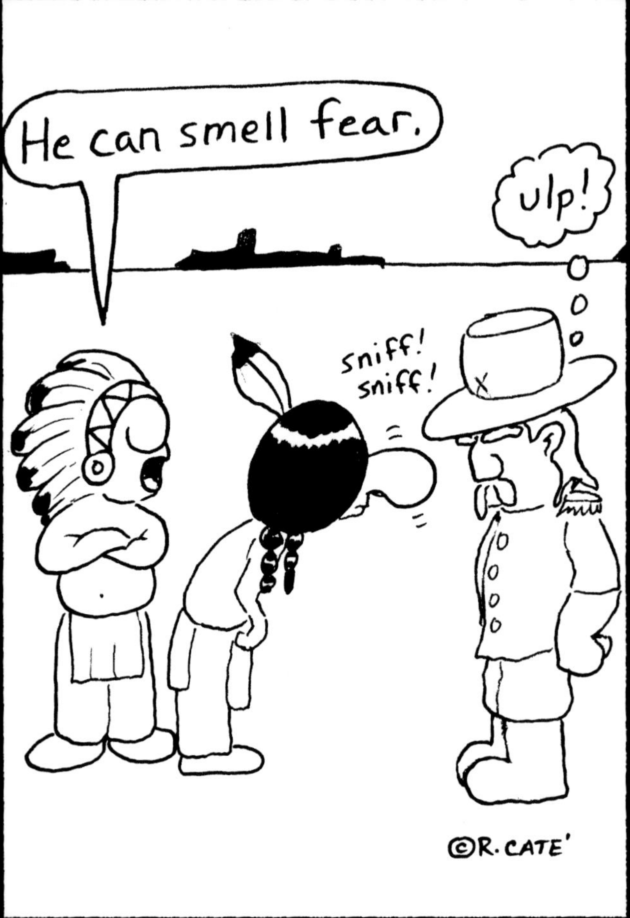
He can smell fear.
ulp!
sniff! sniff!
©R. CATE'

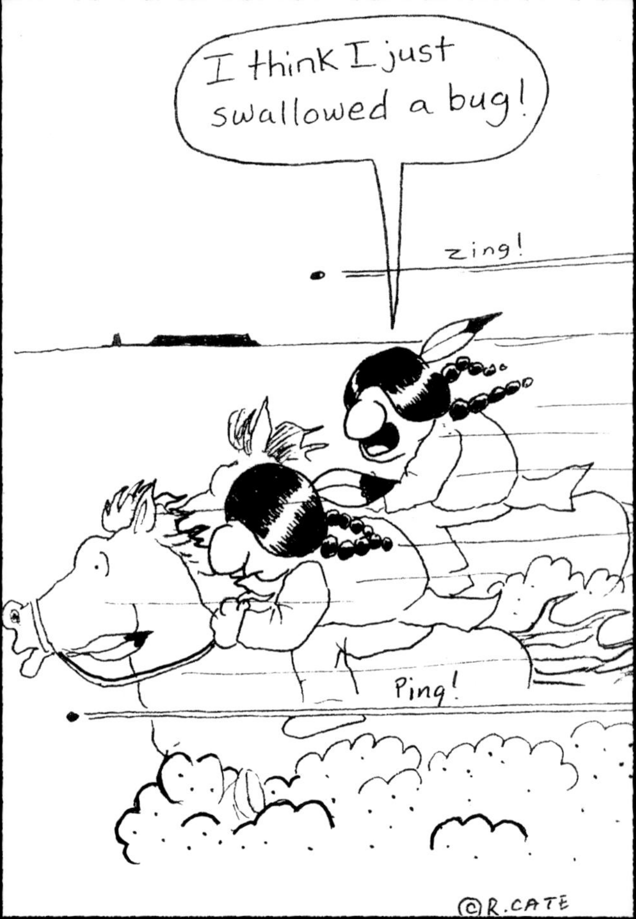
I think I just swallowed a bug!
zing!
Ping!
©R. CATE

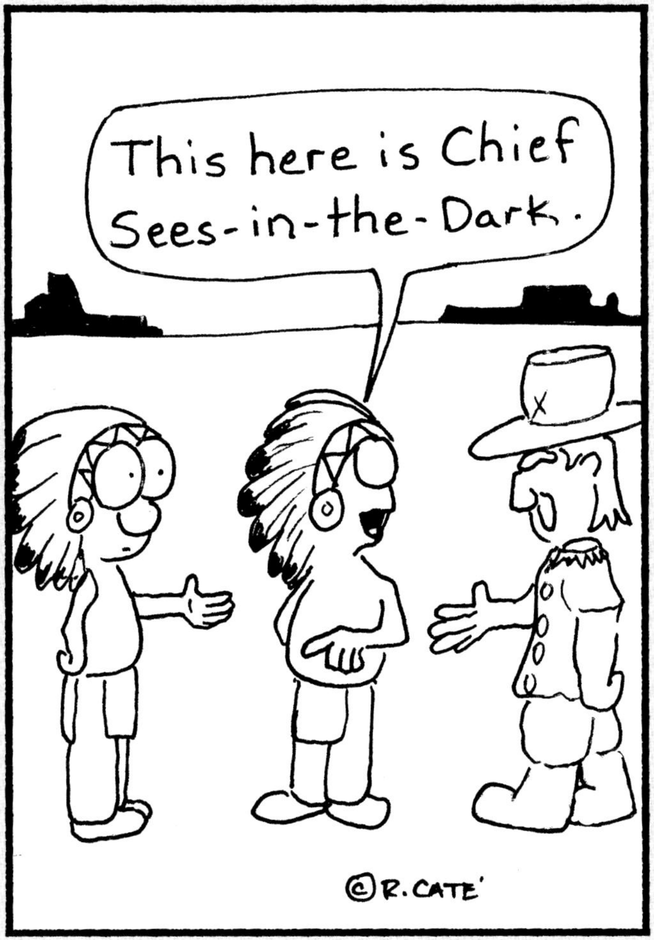
This here is Chief Sees-in-the-Dark.
©R. CATE'

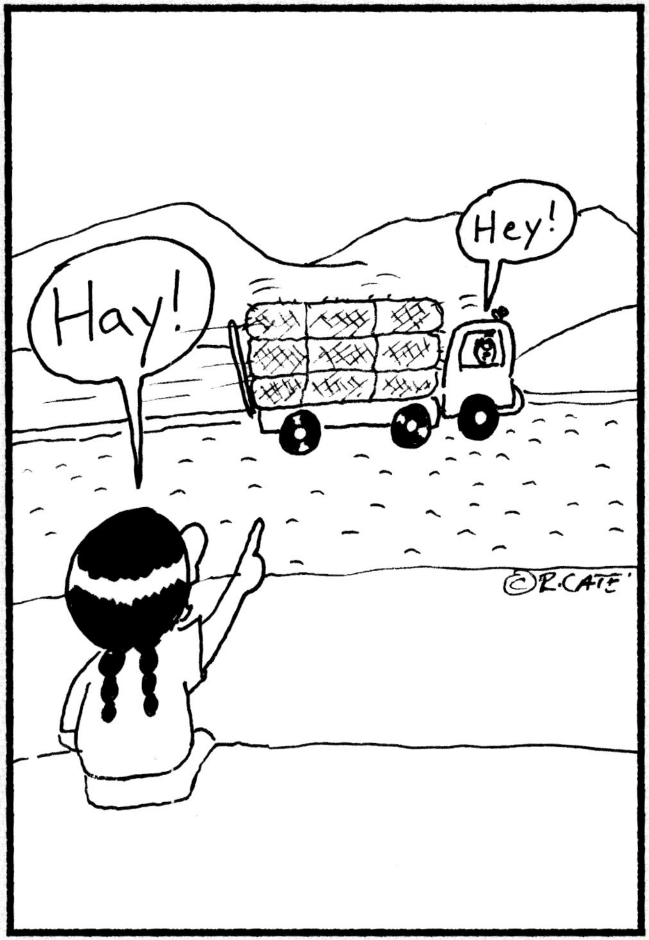
Hay!
Hey!
©R.CATE'

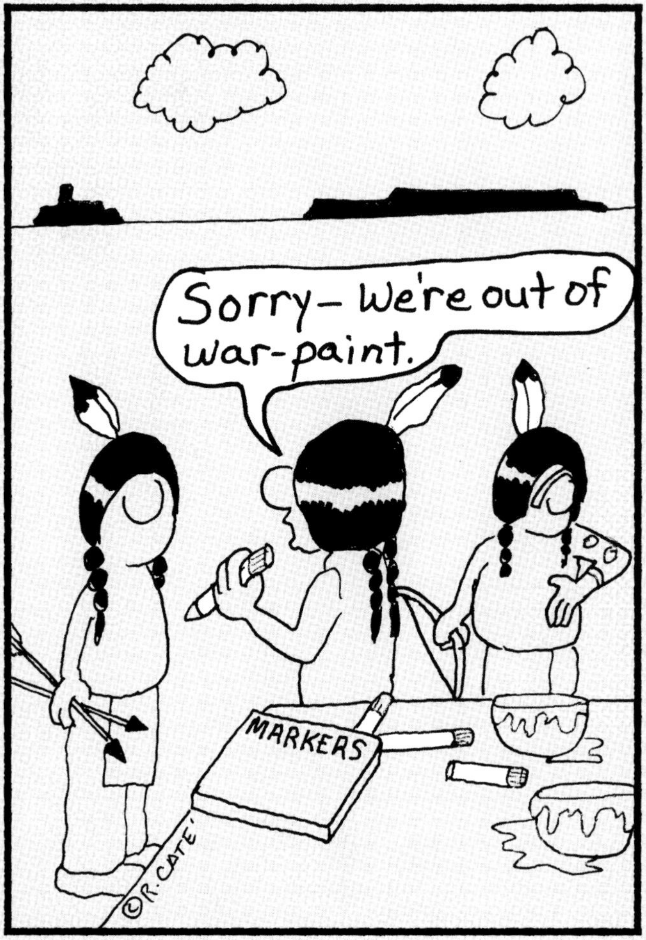
Sorry– We're out of war-paint.
MARKERS
©R.CATE

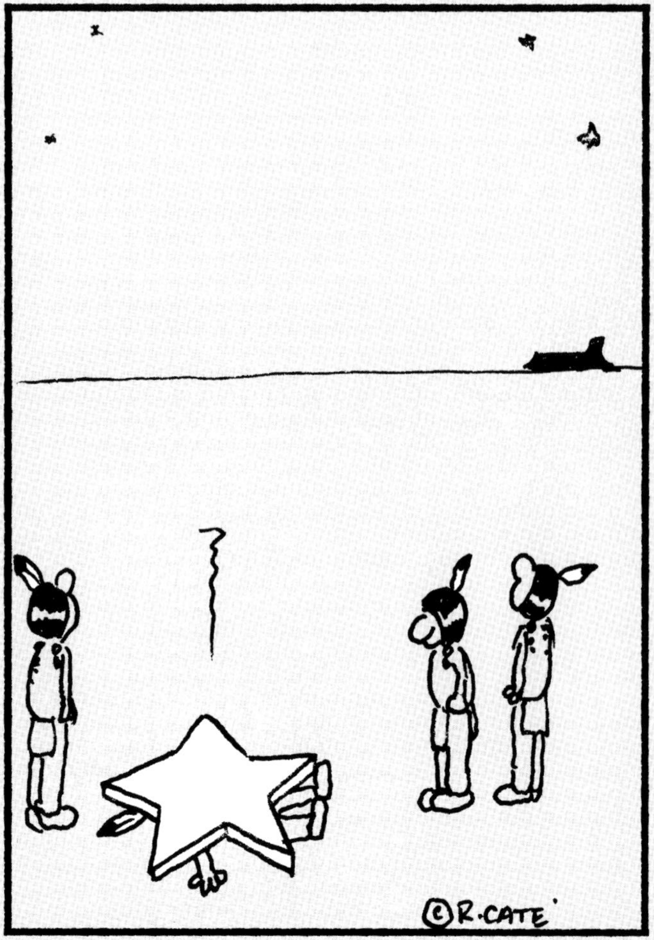
©R.CATE

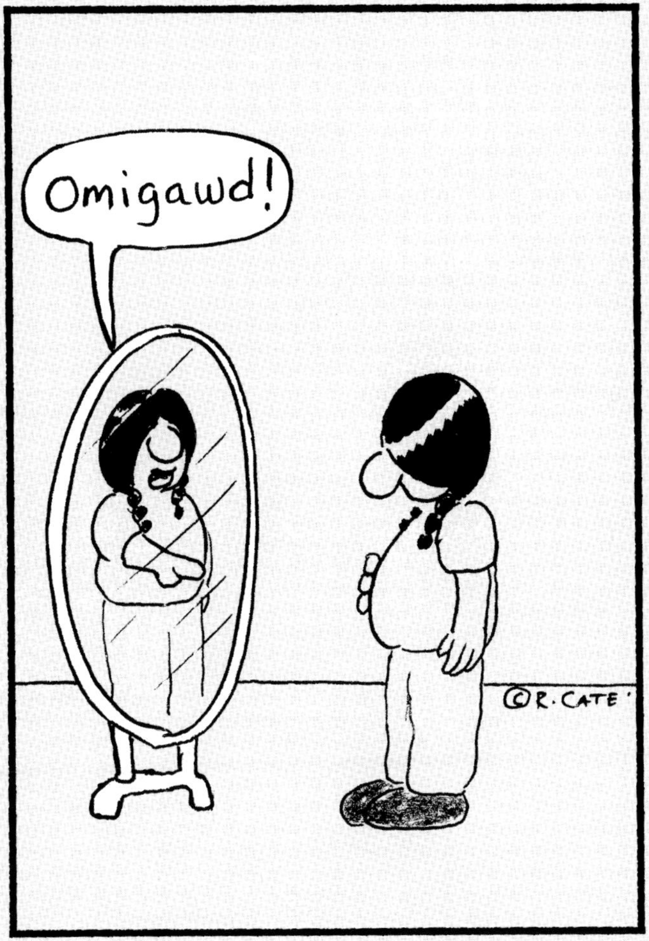
Omigawd!
©R. CATE

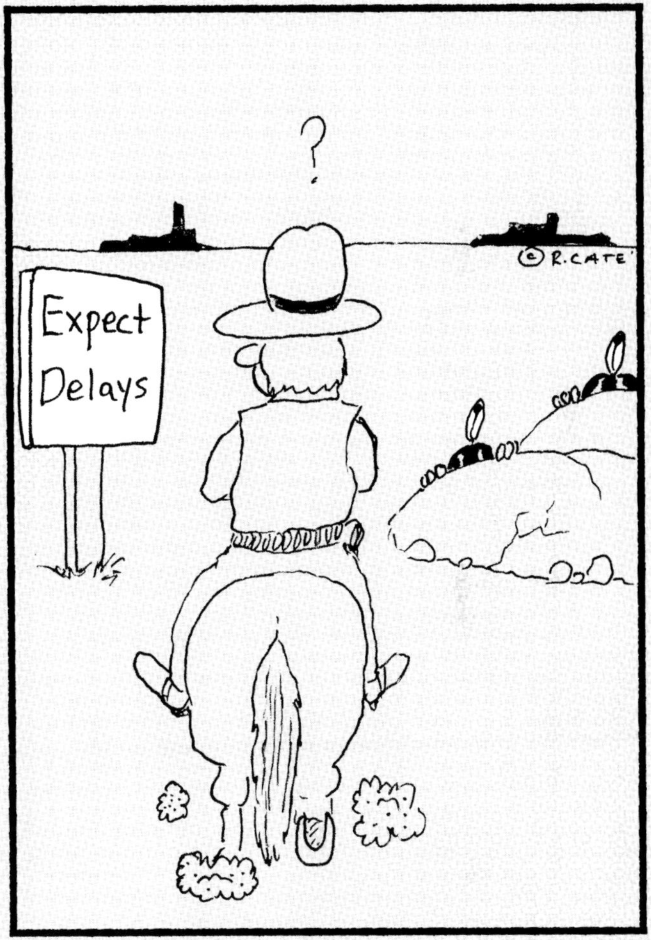
?
©R. CATE
Expect Delays

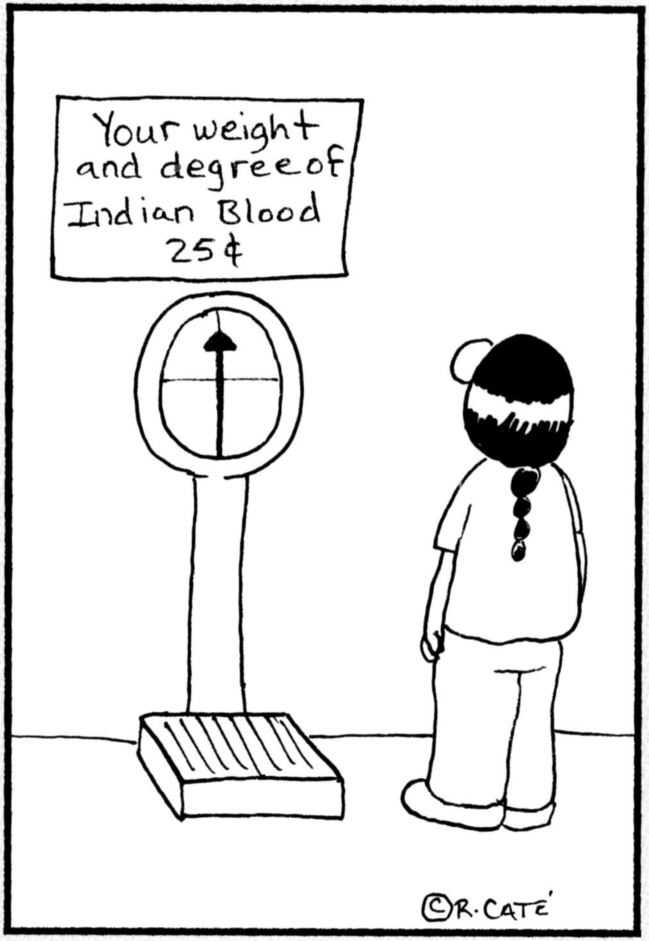
Your weight and degree of Indian Blood 25¢
©R. CATE'

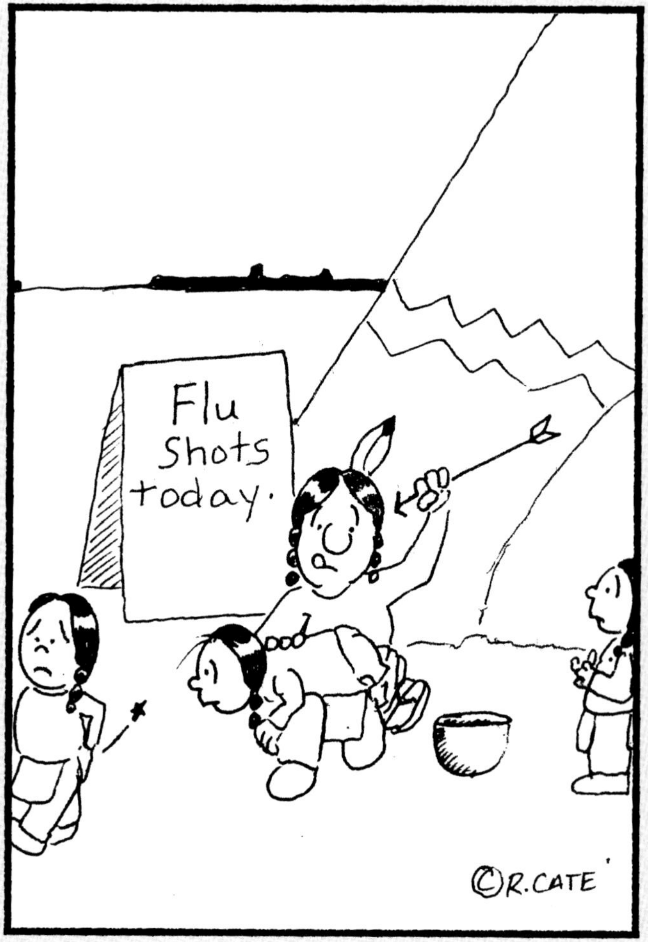
Flu Shots today.
©R. CATE'

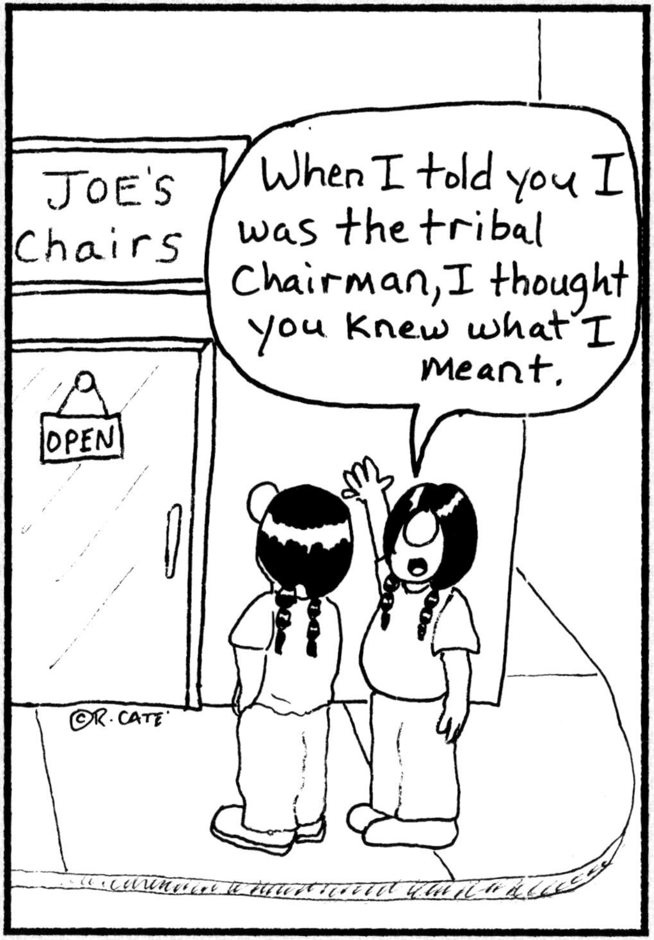
JOE'S Chairs
OPEN
When I told you I was the tribal Chairman, I thought you knew what I meant.
©R. CATE

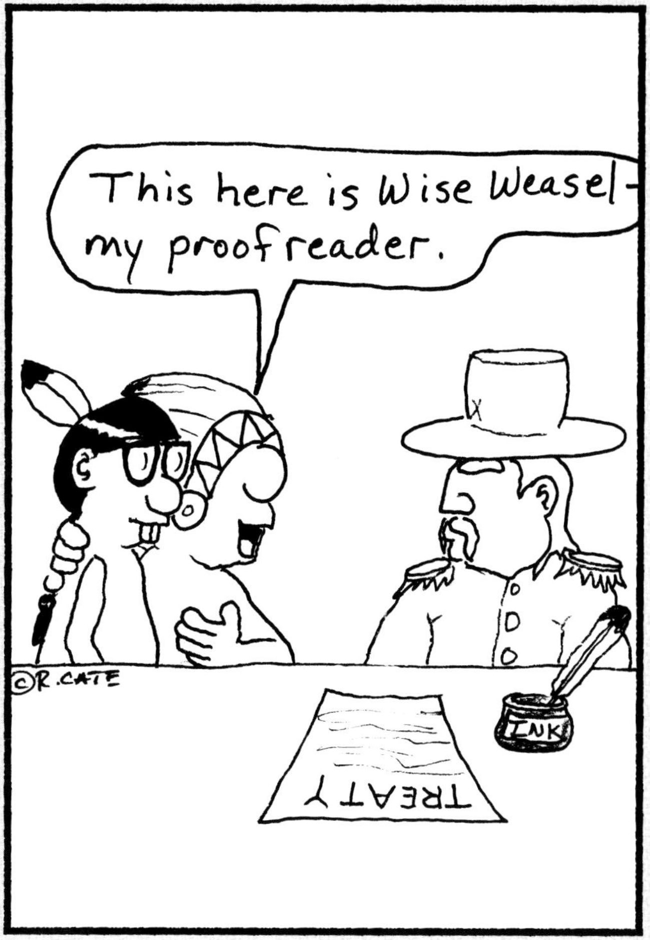
This here is Wise Weasel - my proofreader.
©R. CATE
INK
TREATY

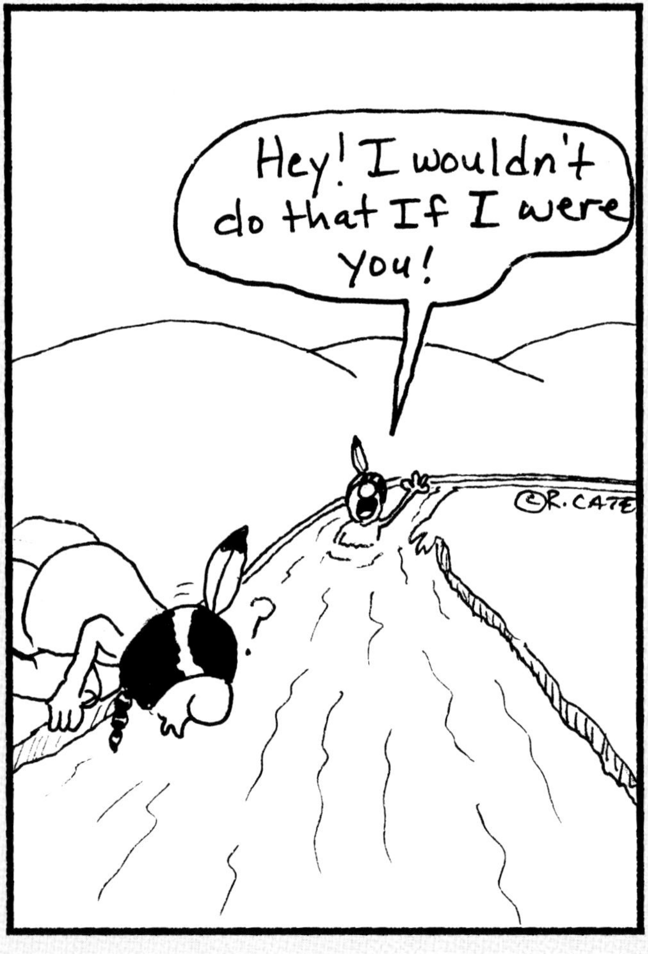
Hey! I wouldn't do that If I were you!
©R.CATE

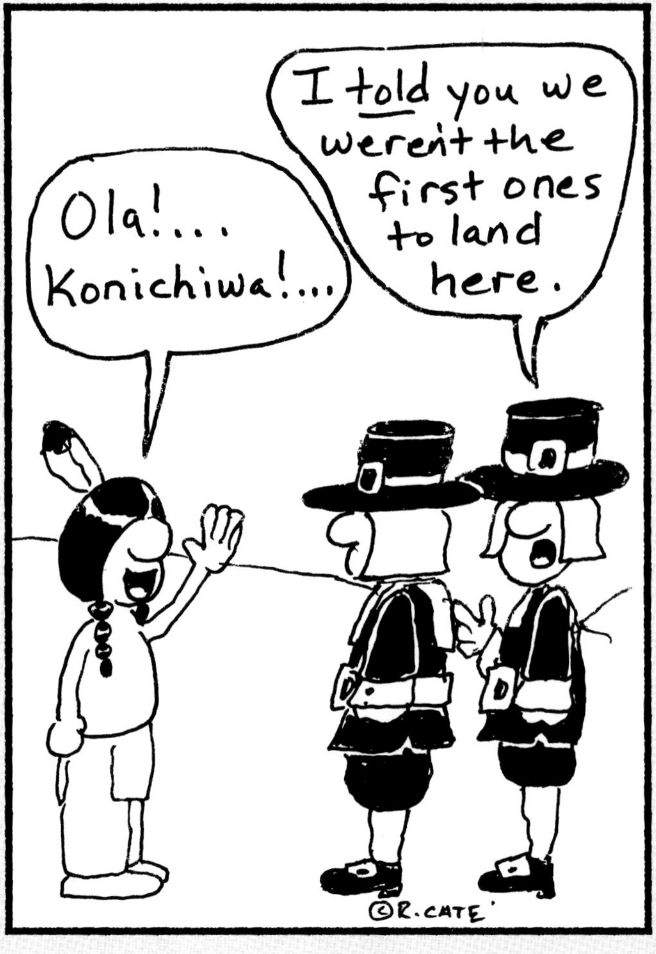
Ola!... Konichiwa!...
I told you we weren't the first ones to land here.
©R.CATE

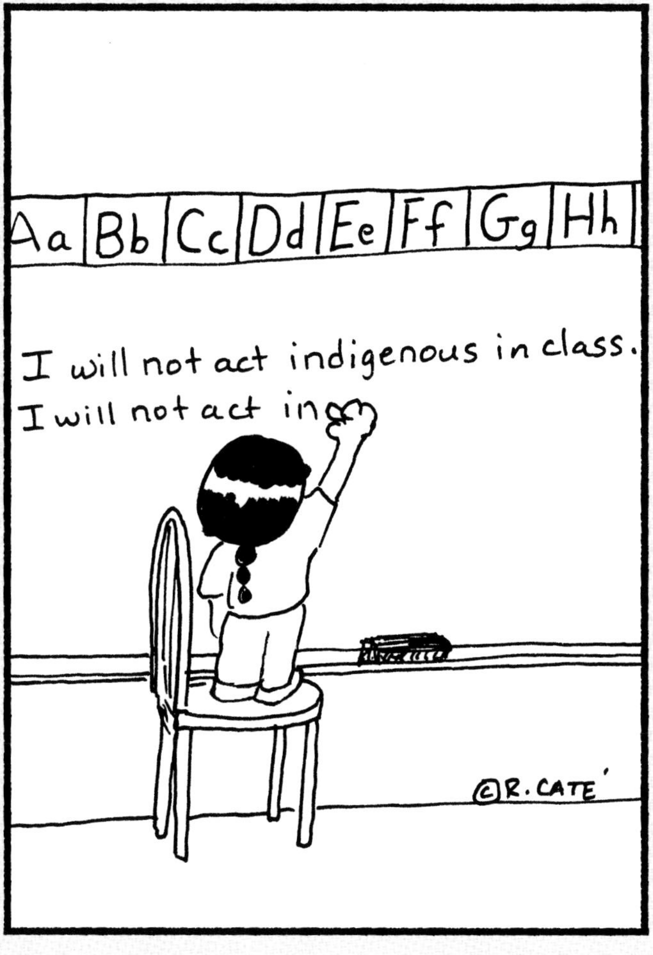
Aa Bb Cc Dd Ee Ff Gg Hh
I will not act indigenous in class.
I will not act in
©R. CATE'

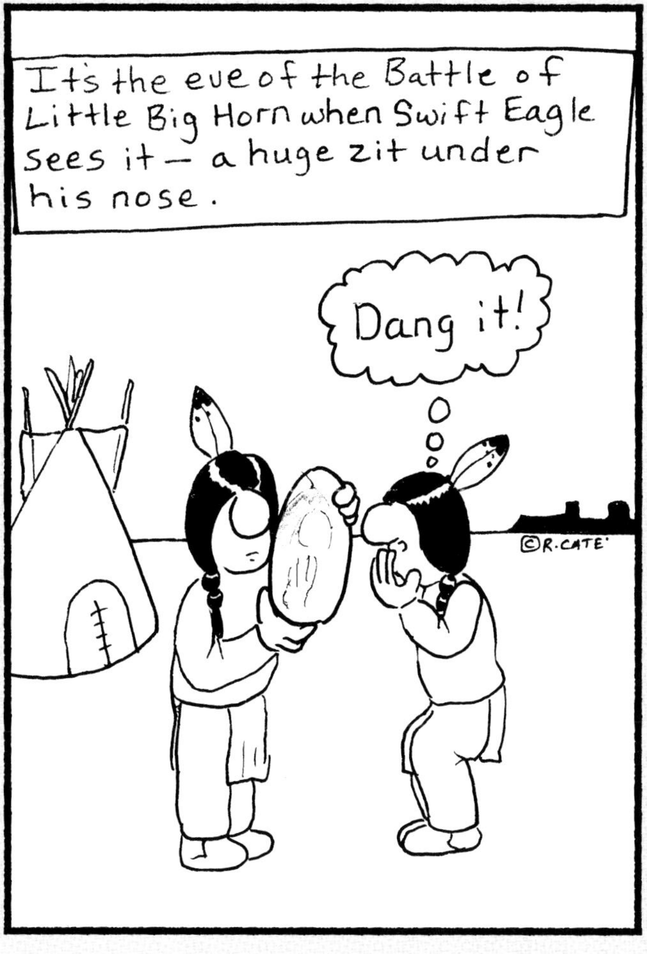
It's the eve of the Battle of Little Big Horn when Swift Eagle sees it — a huge zit under his nose.
Dang it!
©R. CATE'

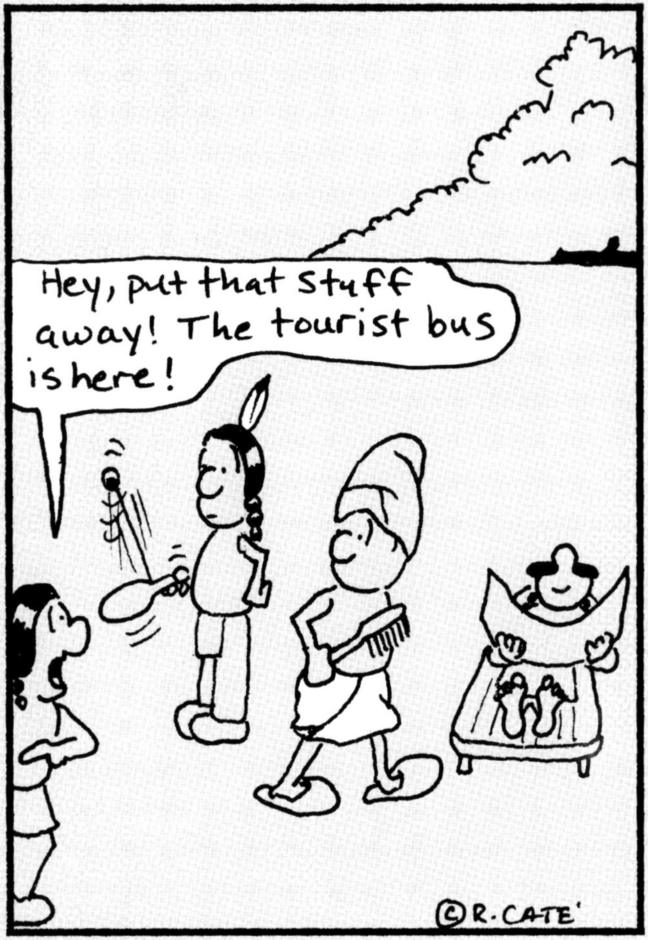
Hey, put that stuff away! The tourist bus is here!
©R. CATE'

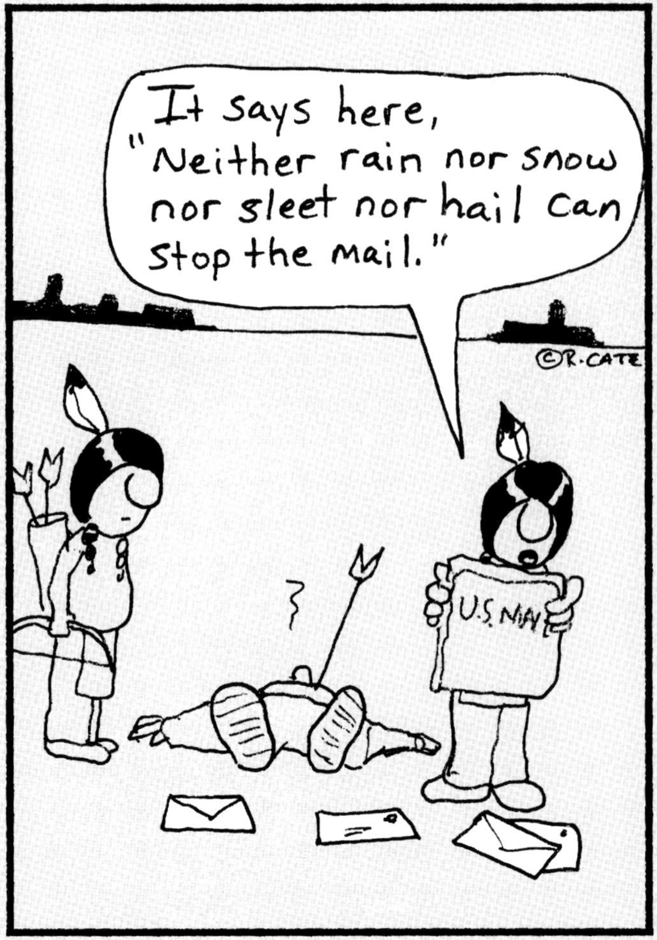
It says here, "Neither rain nor snow nor sleet nor hail can stop the mail."
©R. CATE

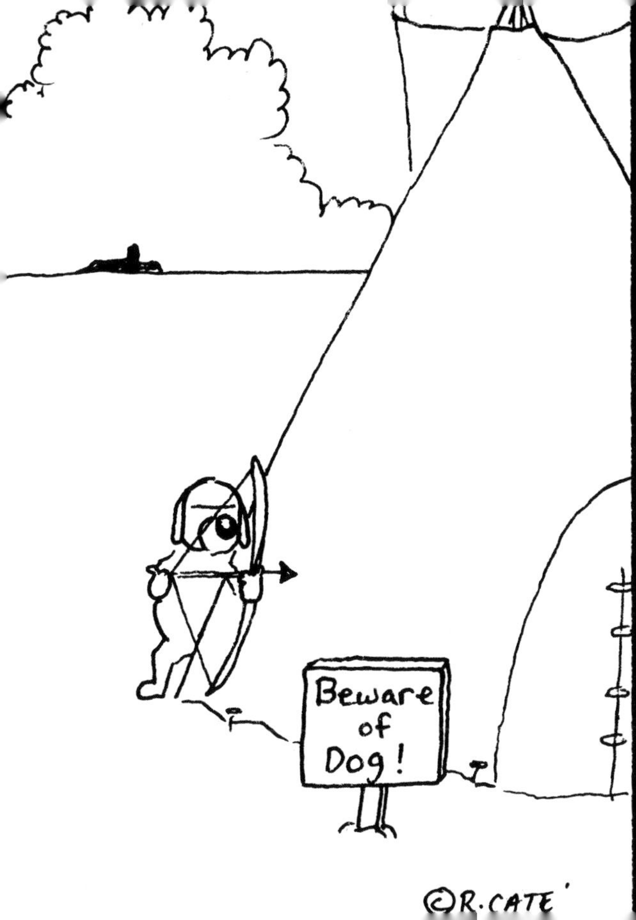
Beware of Dog!
©R.CATE'

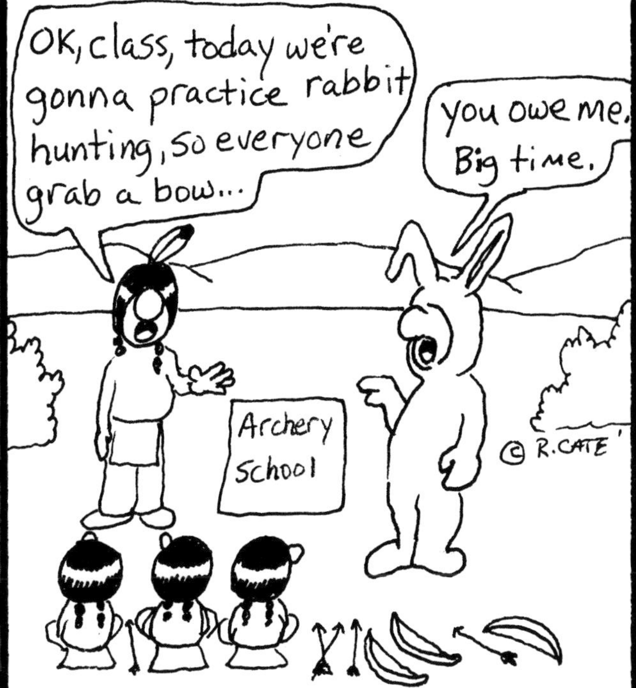
OK, class, today we're gonna practice rabbit hunting, so everyone grab a bow...
you owe me. Big time.
Archery School
© R.CATE'

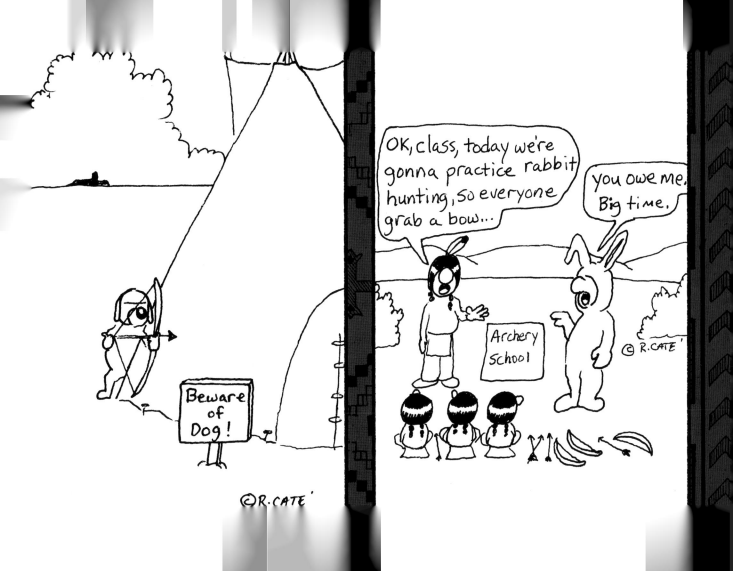

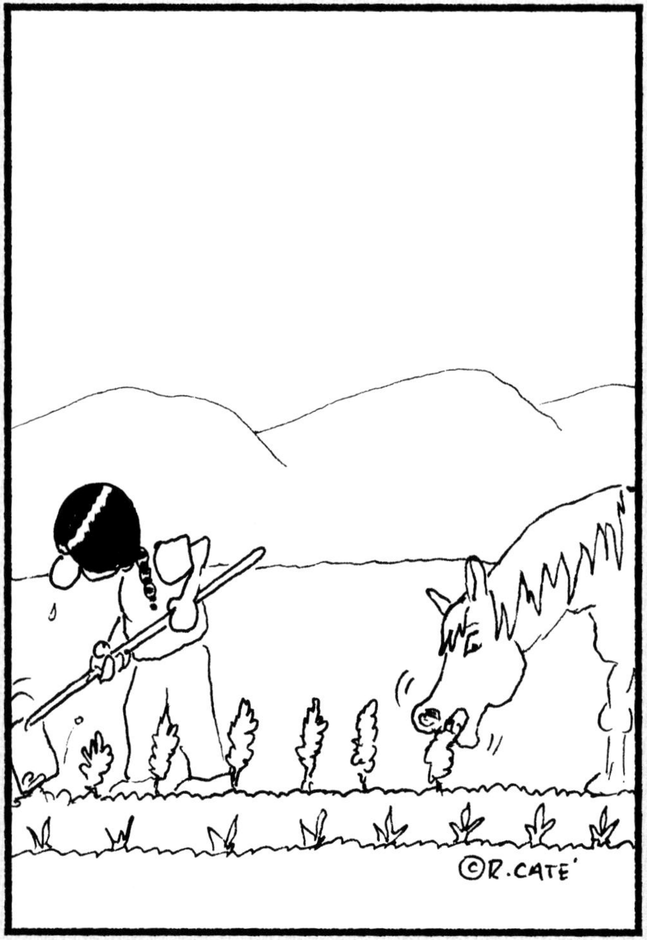
©R.CATE'

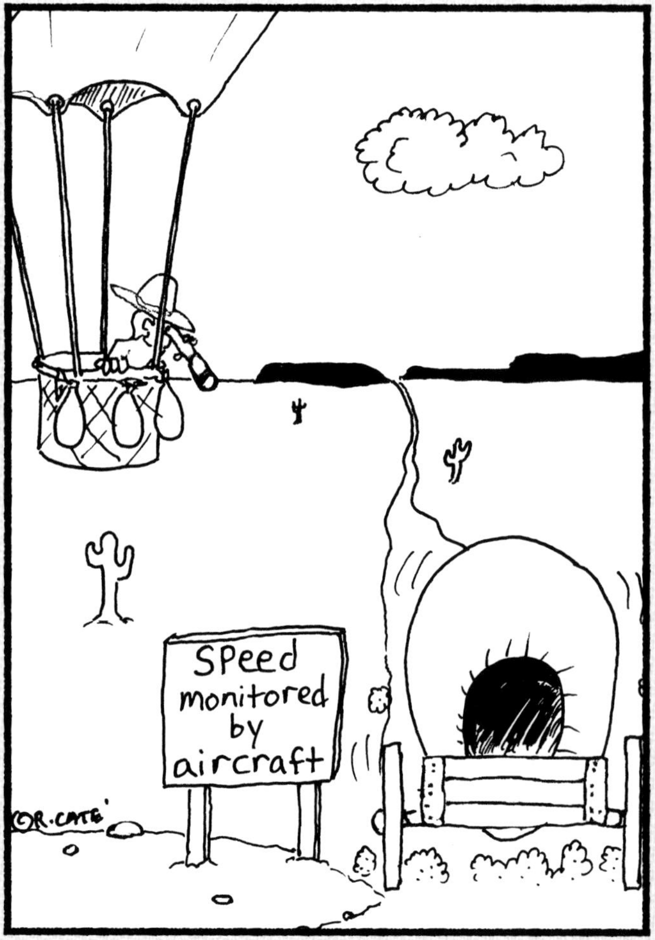
Speed
monitored
by
aircraft
©R.CATE'

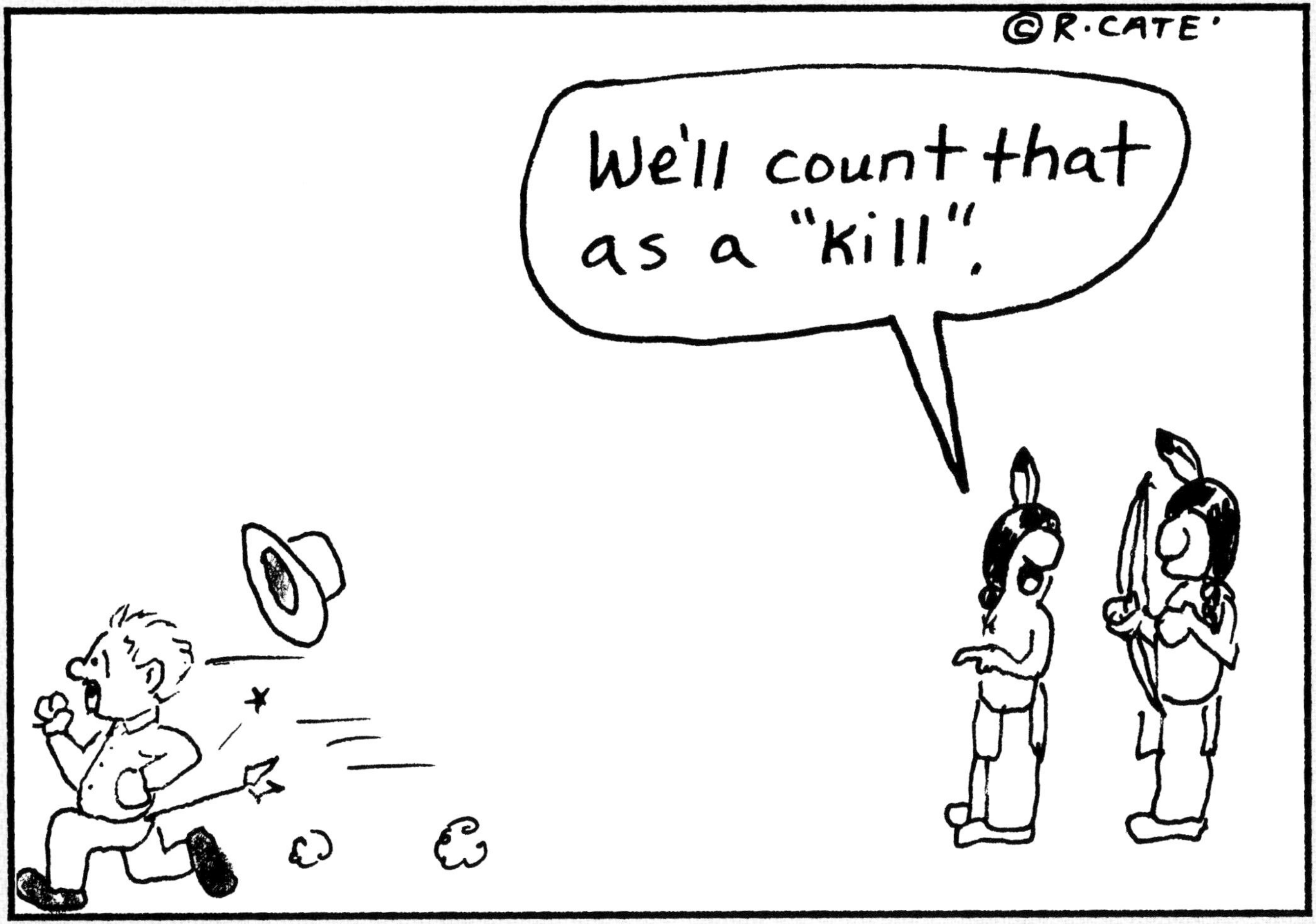
©R·CATE·
We'll count that as a "kill".

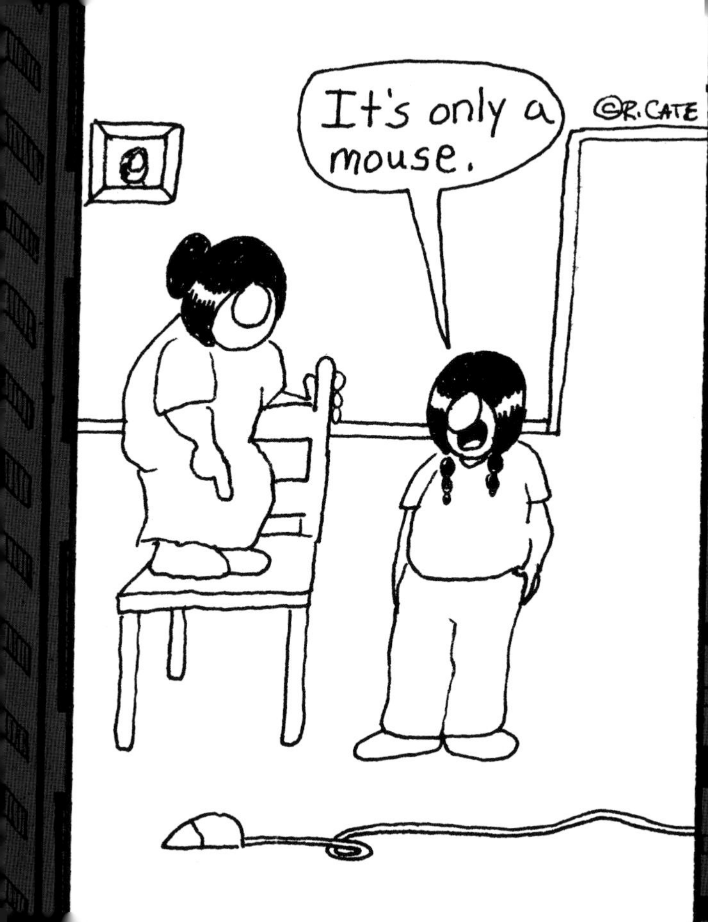

It's only a mouse.
©R.CATE

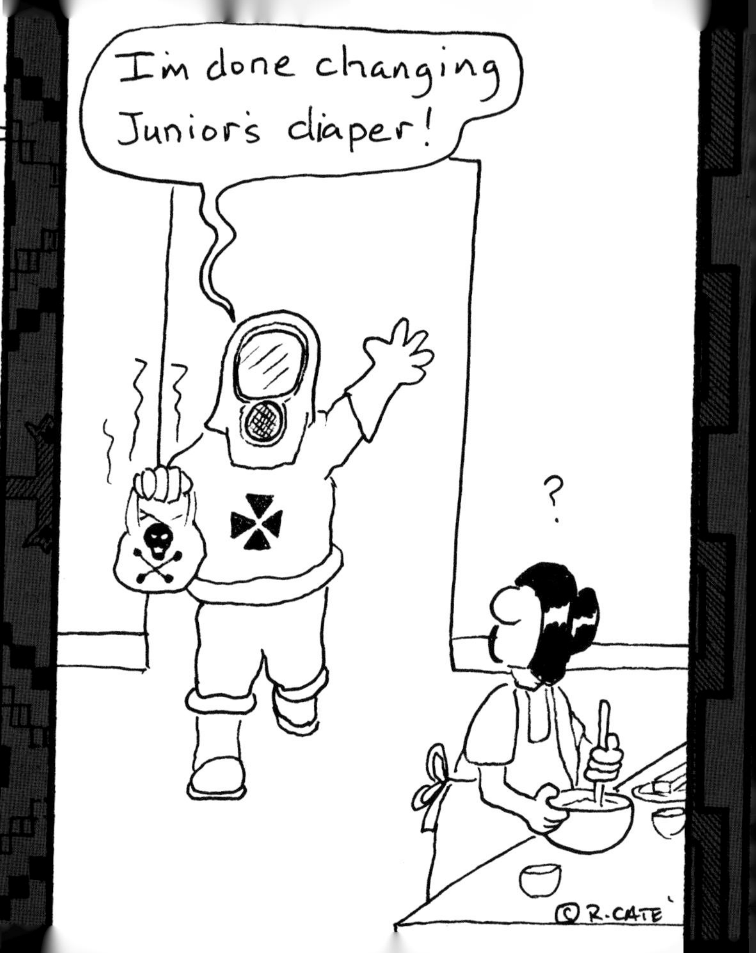

I'm done changing Junior's diaper!
?
© R.CATE

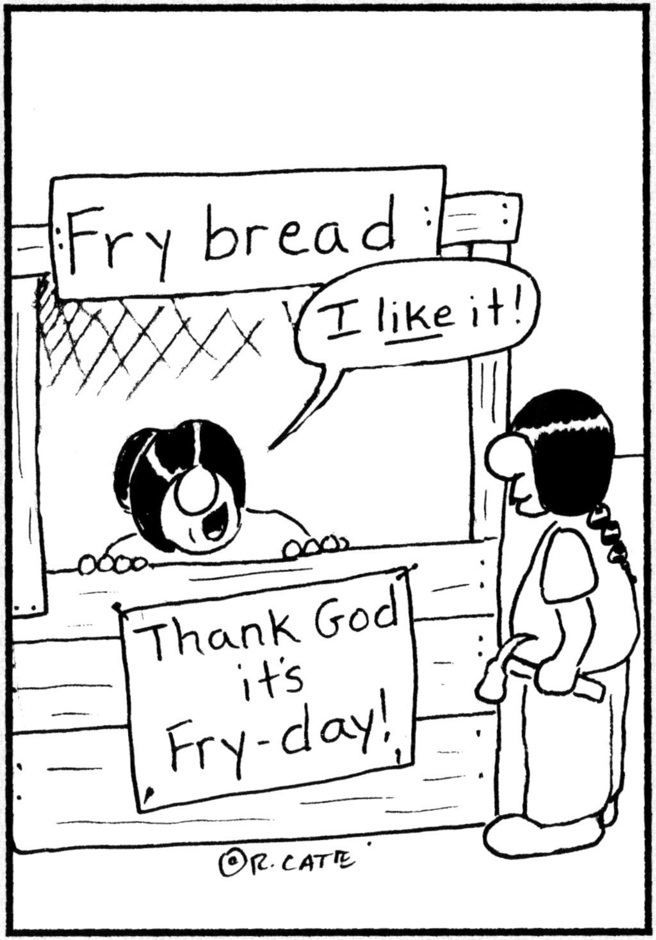
Fry bread
I like it!
Thank God it's Fry-day!
©R. CATE'

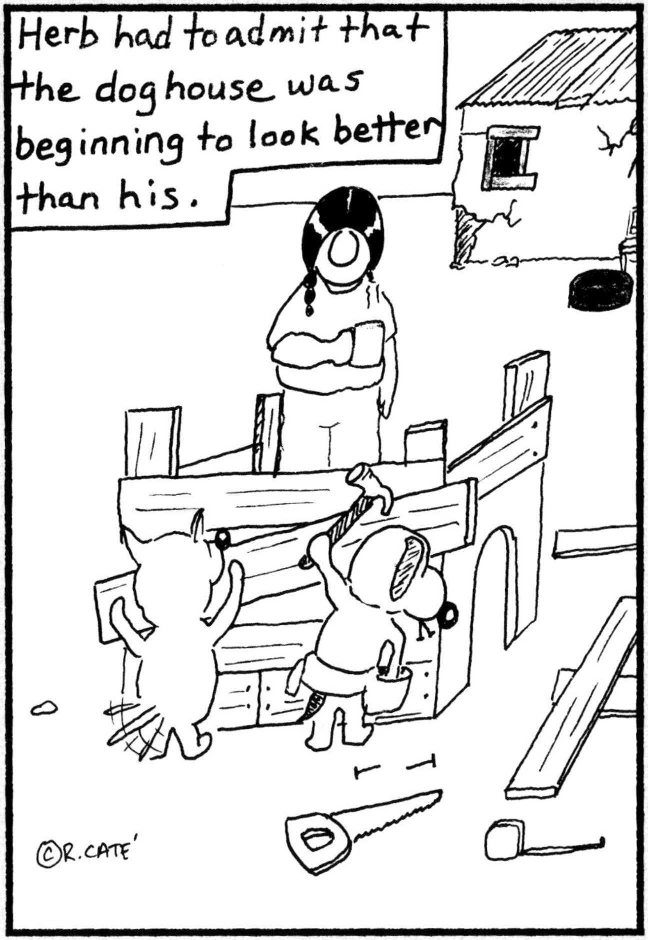
Herb had to admit that the dog house was beginning to look better than his.
©R. CATE'

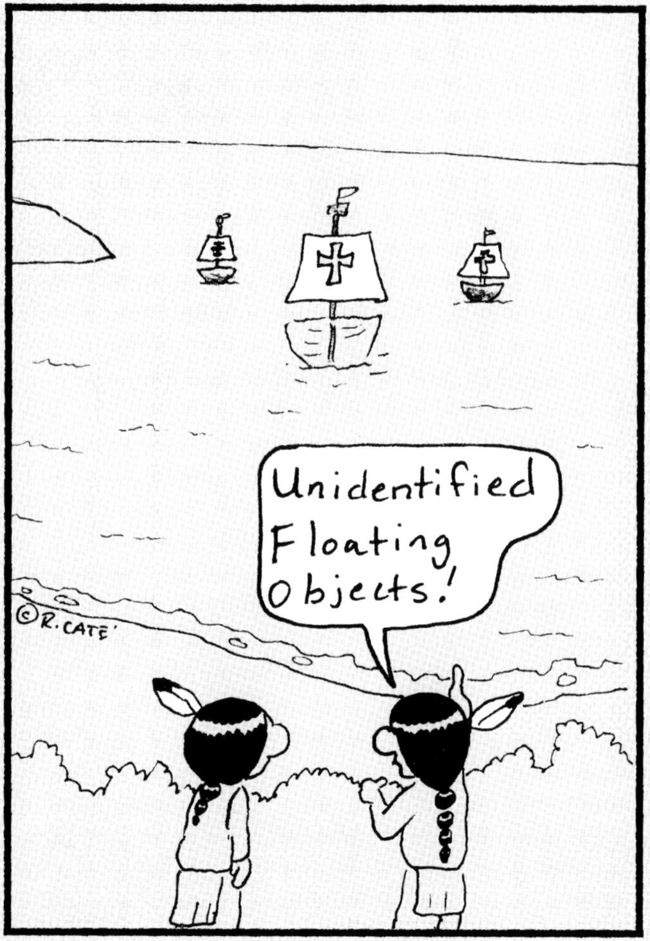
Unidentified Floating Objects!
©R. CATE

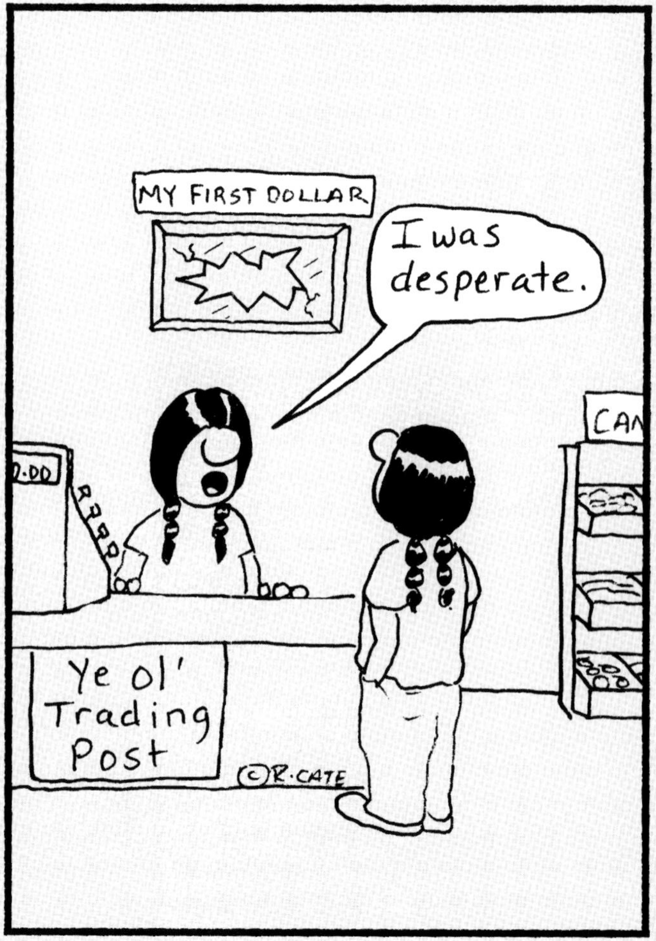
MY FIRST DOLLAR
I was desperate.
Ye ol' Trading Post
©R.CATE

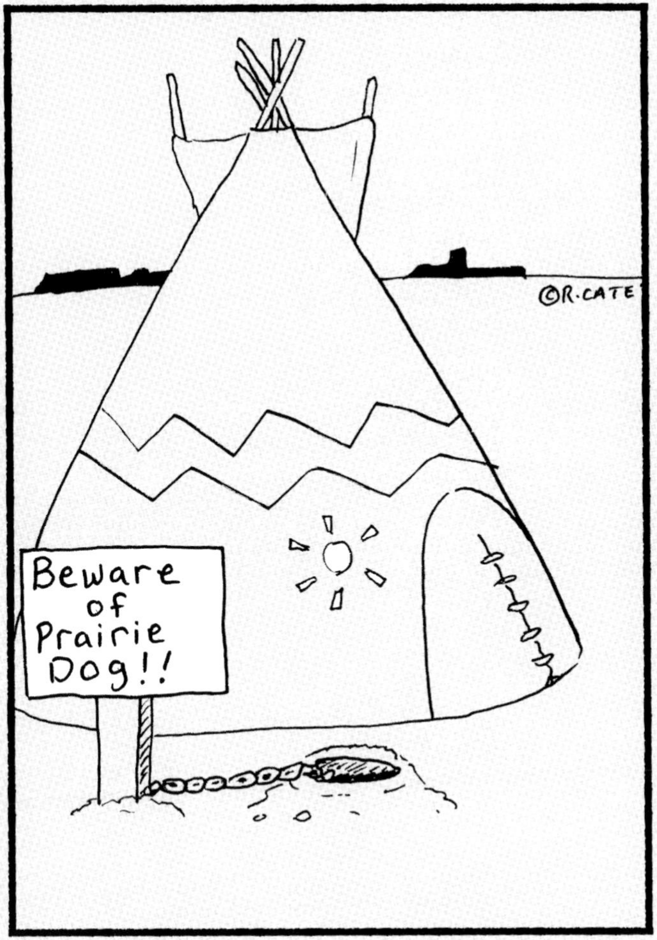
©R.CATE'
Beware of Prairie Dog!!

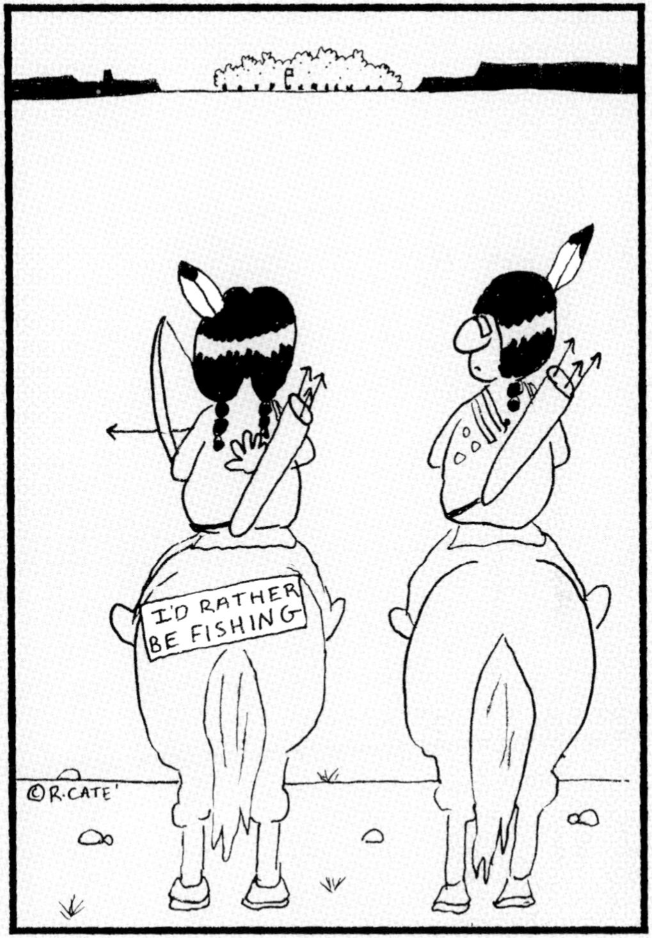
I'D RATHER BE FISHING
©R.CATE'

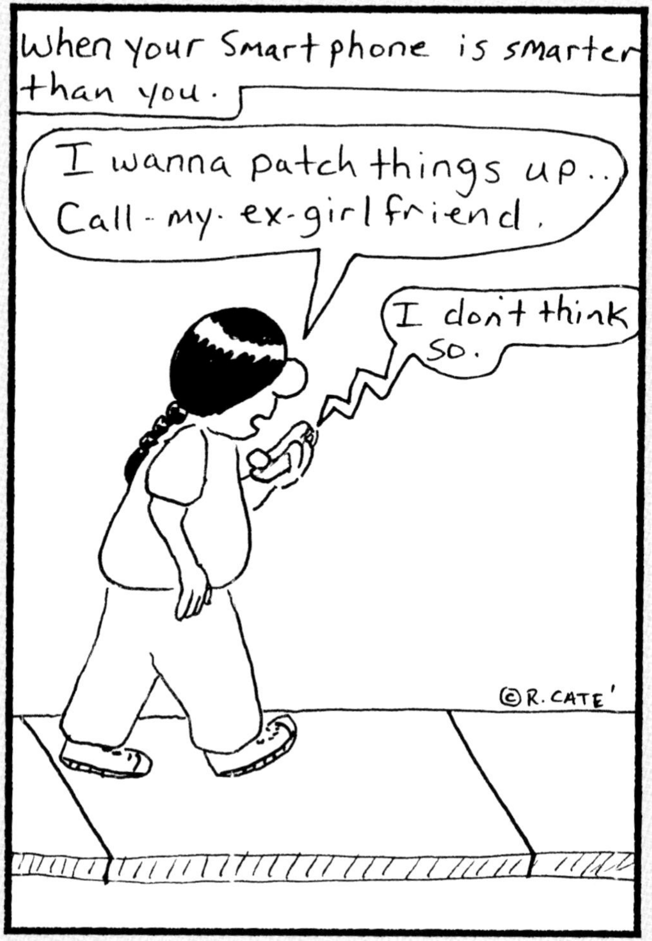
When your Smart phone is smarter than you.
I wanna patch things up.. Call - my - ex - girlfriend.
I don't think so.
©R. CATE'

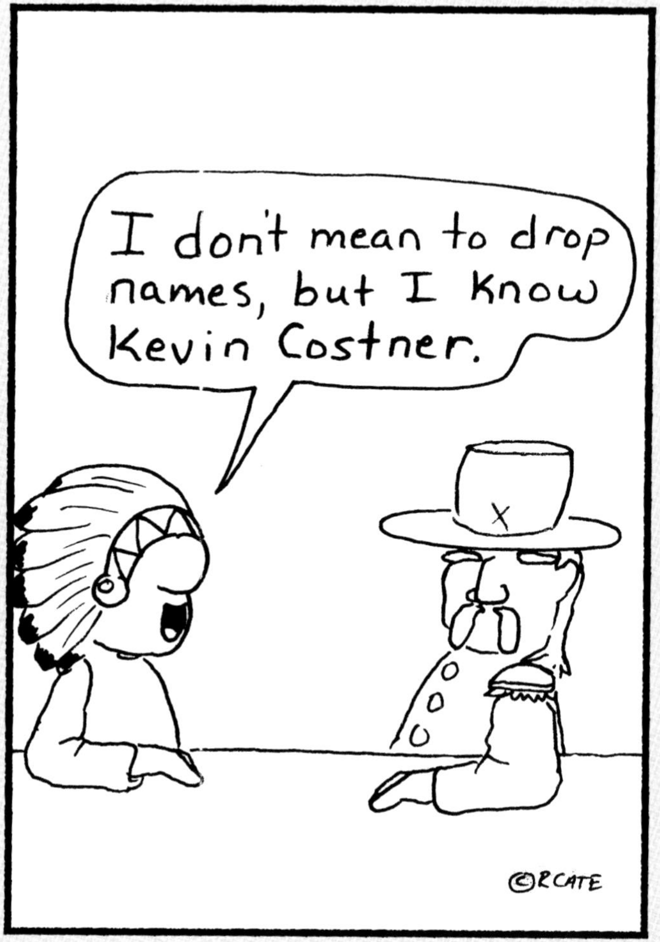
I don't mean to drop names, but I know Kevin Costner.
©RCATE

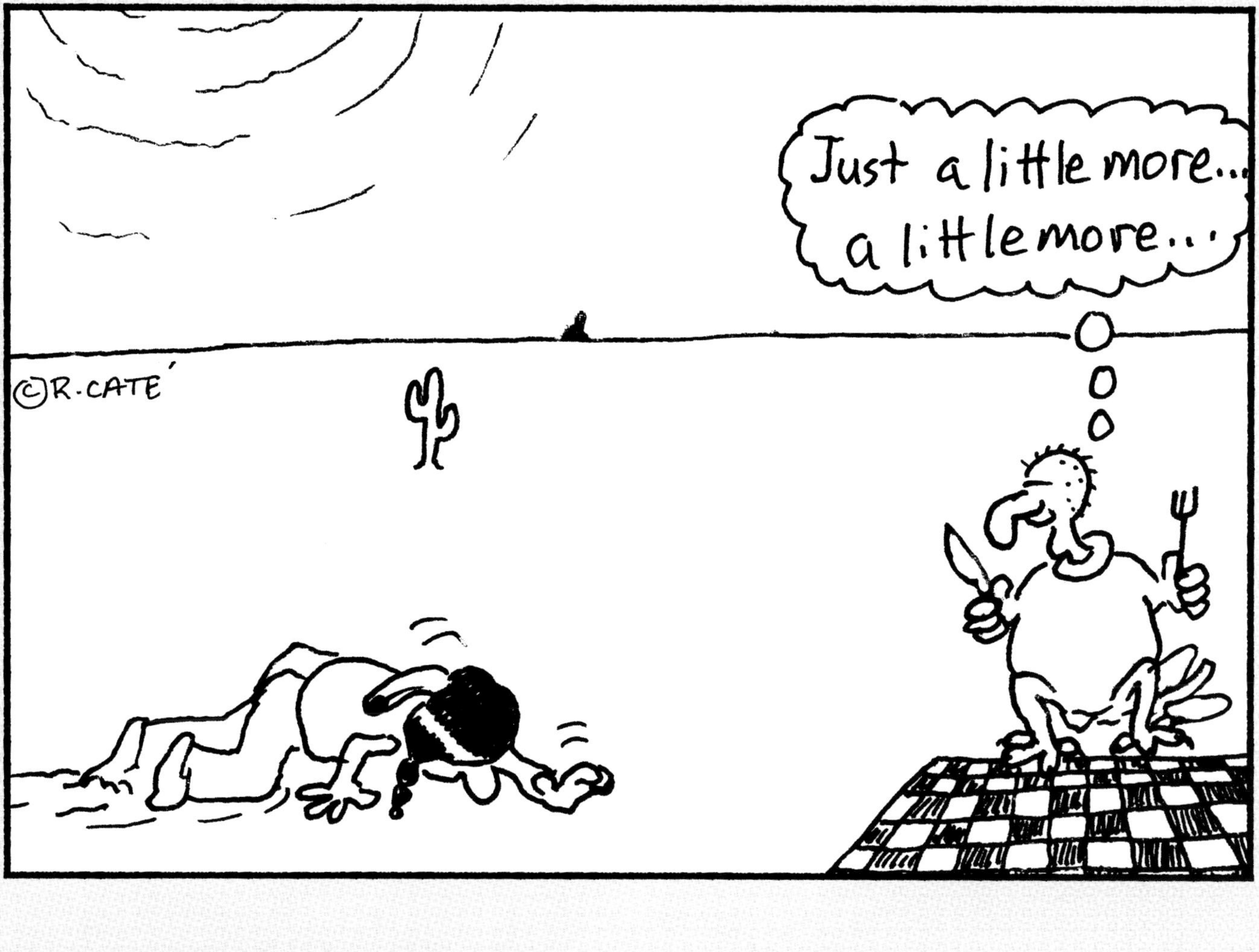
Just a little more...
a little more...
©R. CATE´

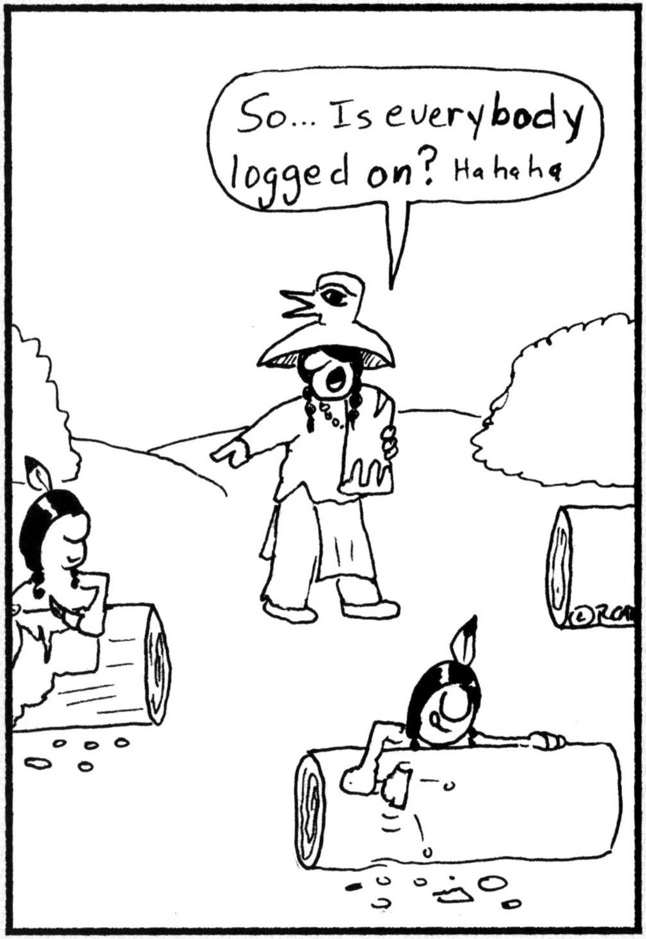
So... Is everybody logged on? Hahaha
©RCATE

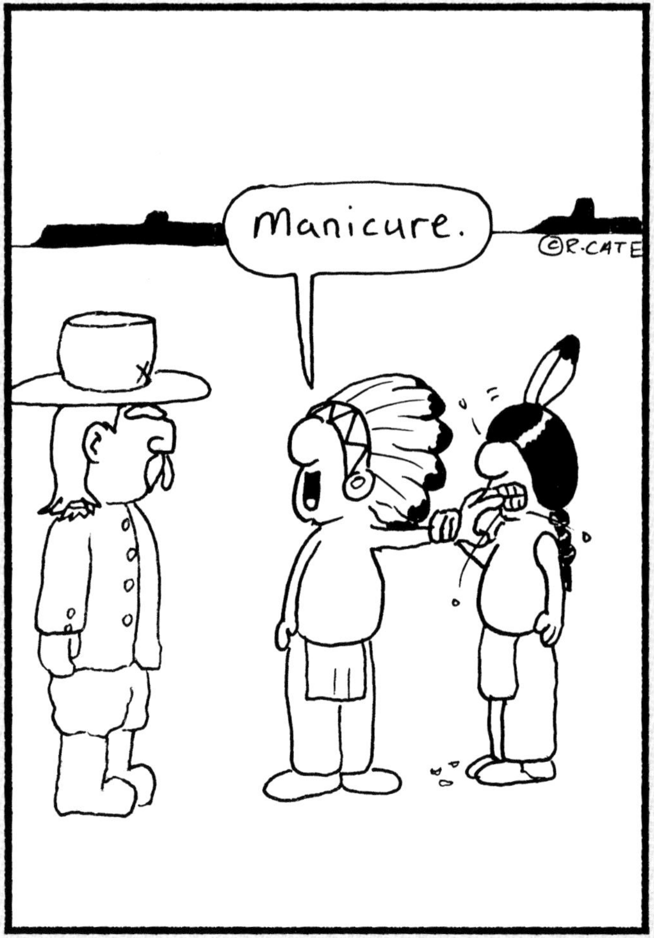
Manicure.
©R.CATE

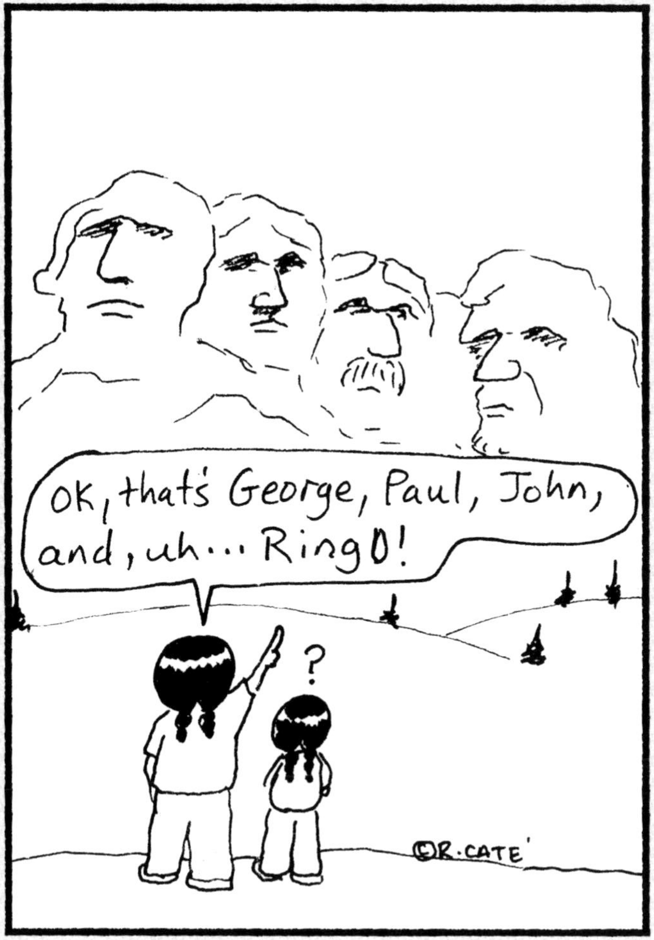
OK, that's George, Paul, John, and, uh... RingO!
?
©R. CATE'

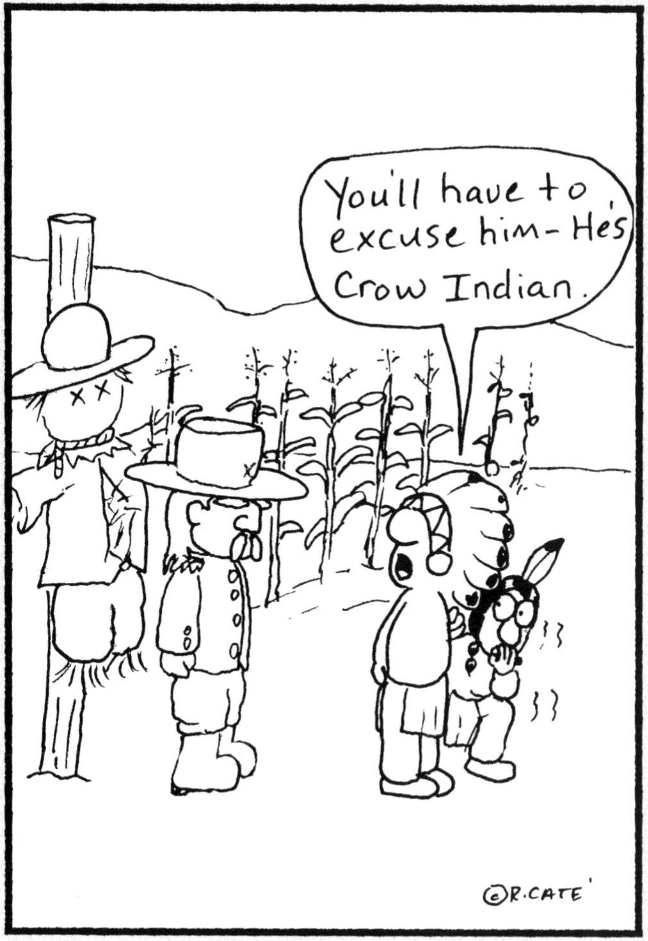
You'll have to excuse him- He's Crow Indian.
©R. CATE'

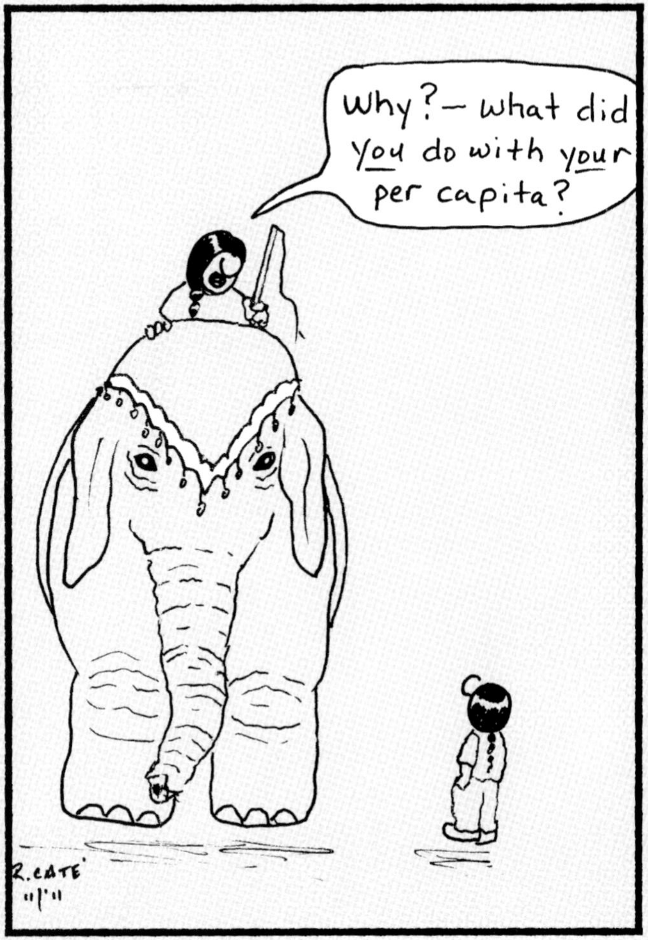
Why?— what did you do with your per capita?
R. CATE' 11|'11

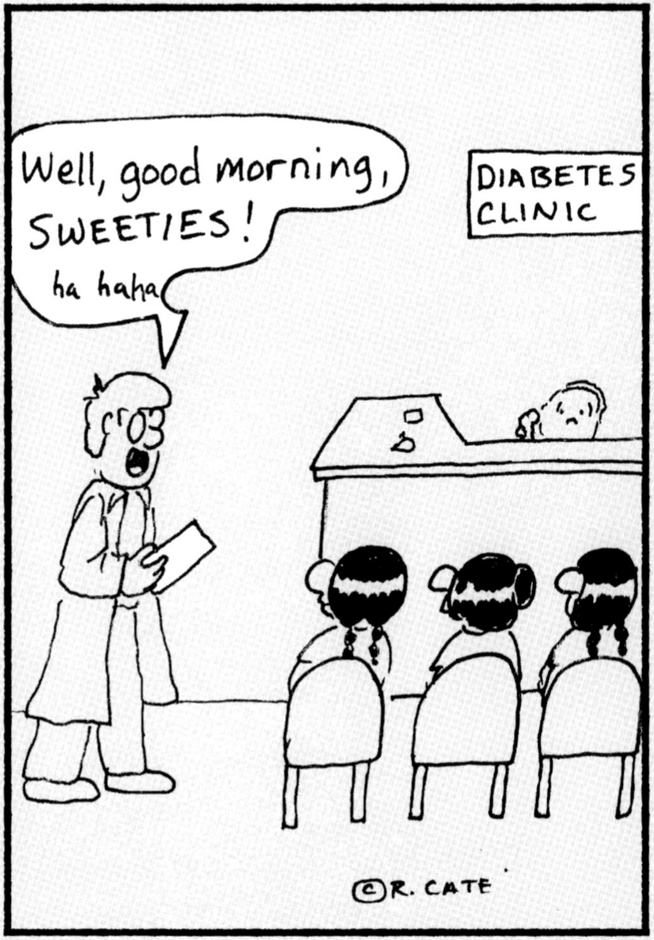
Well, good morning, SWEETIES! ha haha
DIABETES CLINIC
©R. CATE'

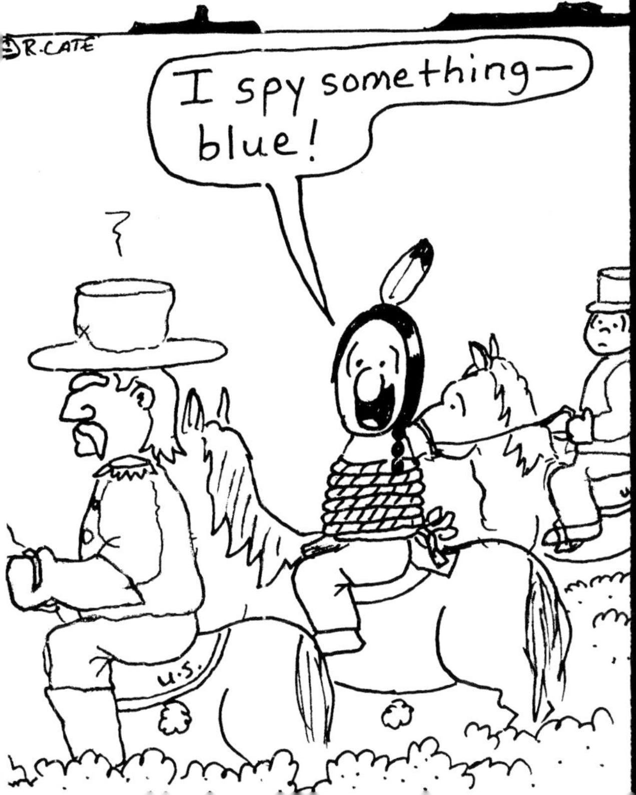
R.CATE
I spy something— blue!
?

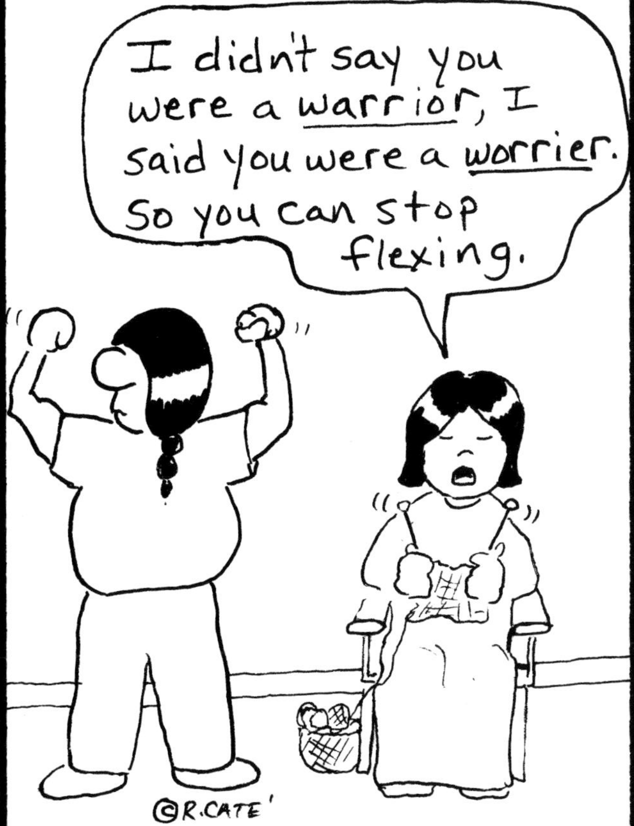
I didn't say you were a warrior, I said you were a worrier. So you can stop flexing.
©R.CATE

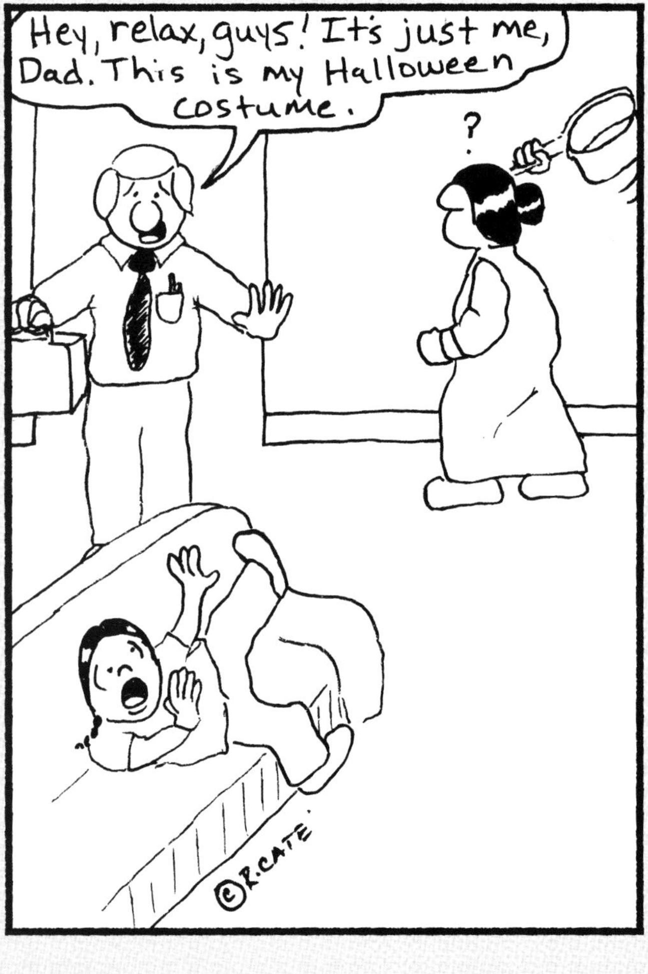
Hey, relax, guys! It's just me, Dad. This is my Halloween costume.
?
©R.CATE

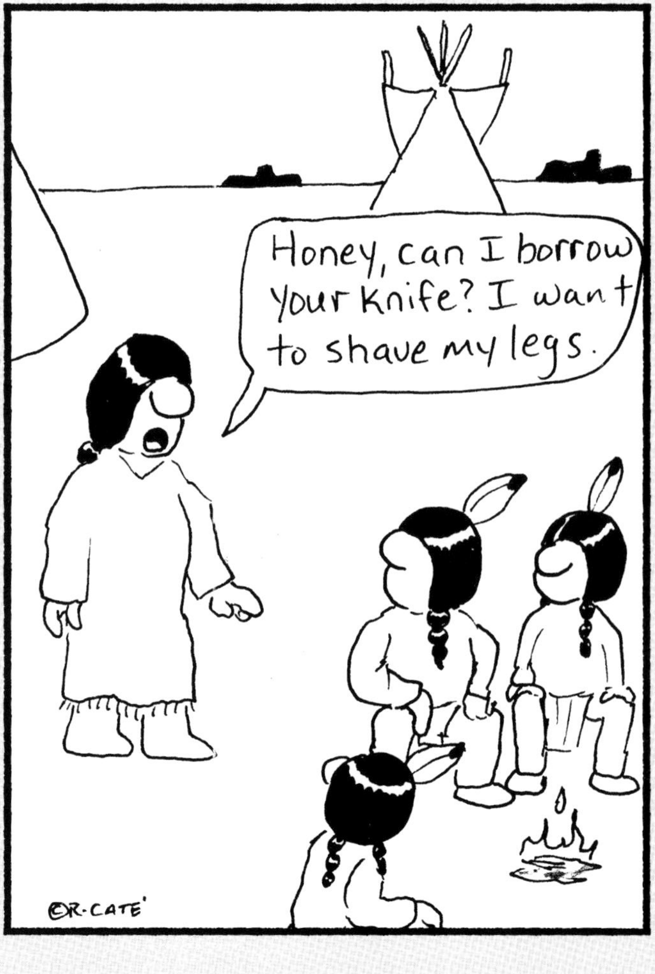
Honey, can I borrow your knife? I want to shave my legs.
©R.CATE

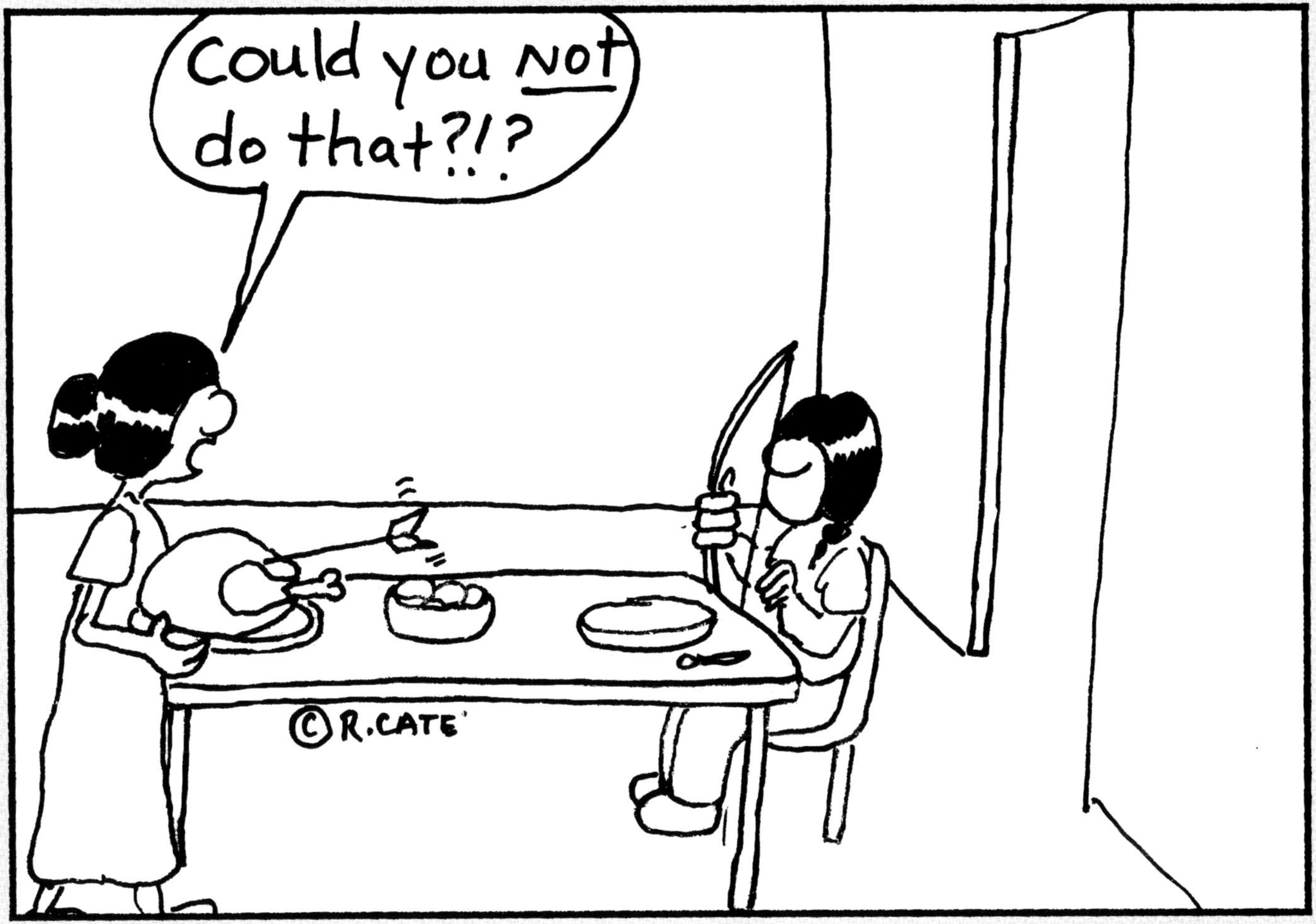
Could you NOT do that?!?
©R.CATE

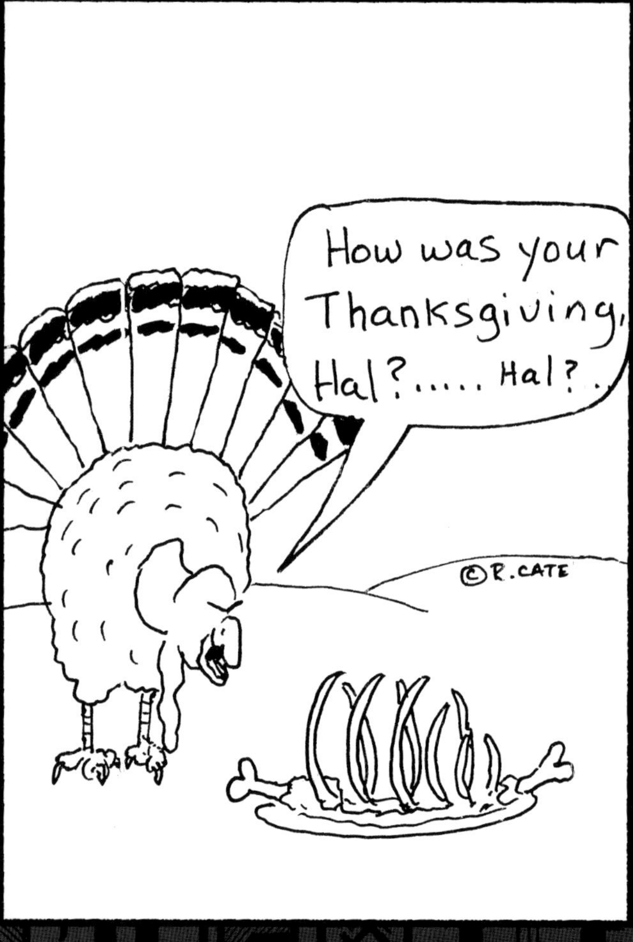
How was your Thanksgiving, Hal?..... Hal?..
©R.CATE

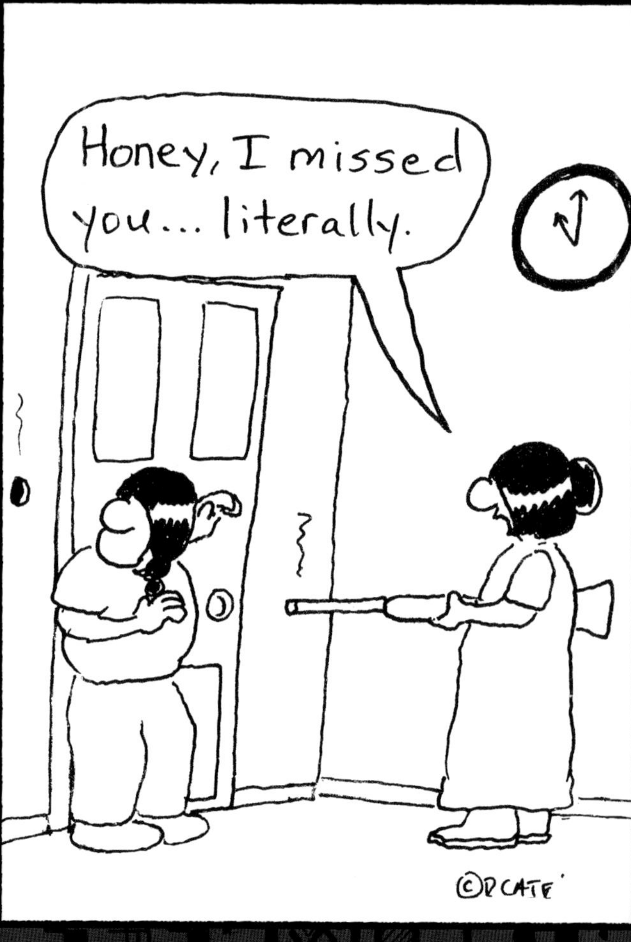
Honey, I missed you... literally.
©R.CATE

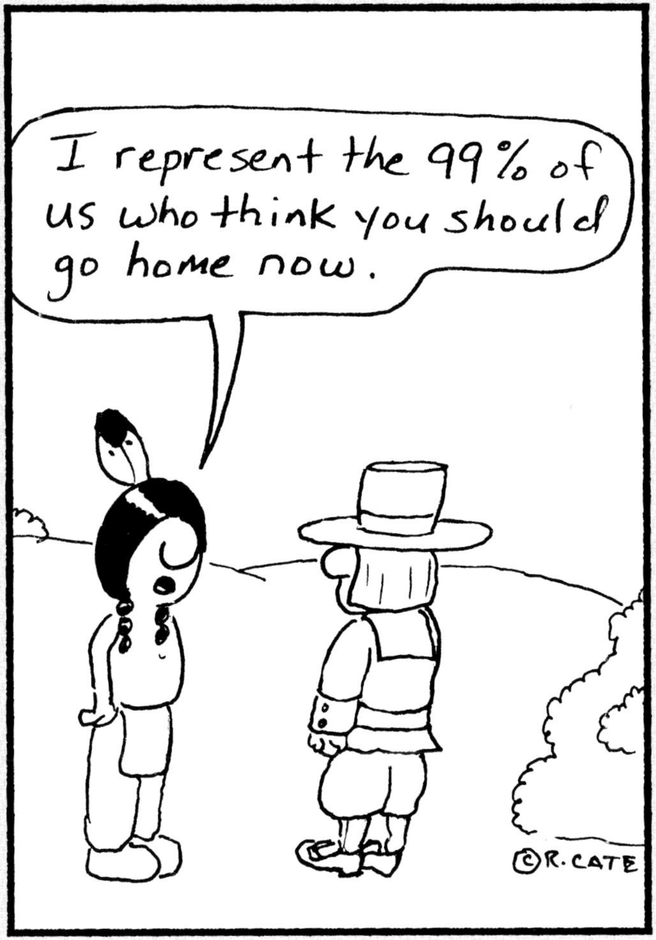
I represent the 99% of us who think you should go home now.
©R. CATE

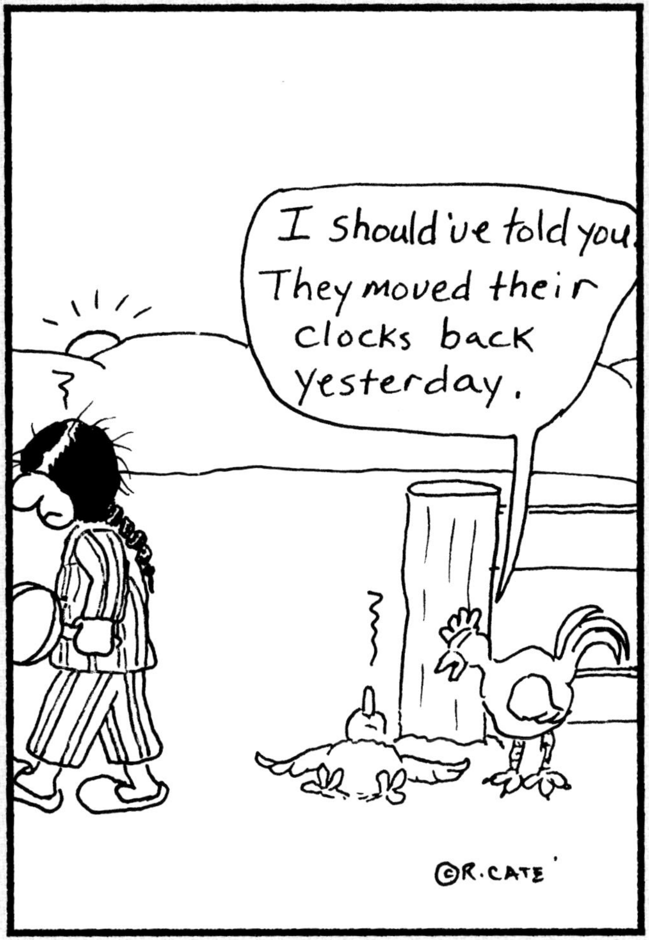
I should've told you. They moved their clocks back yesterday.
©R. CATE

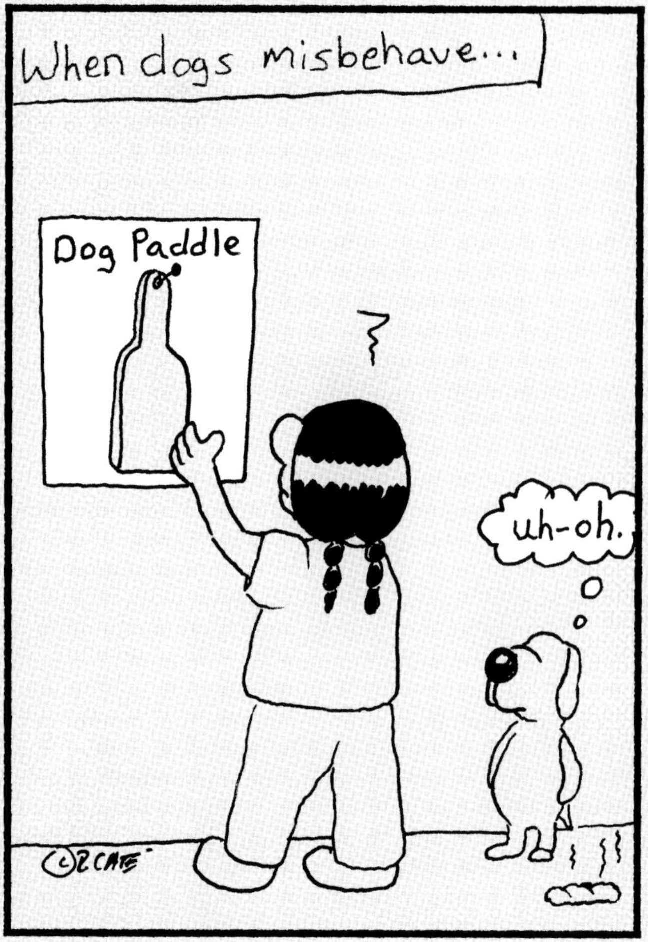
When dogs misbehave...
Dog Paddle
uh-oh.
©R.CATE

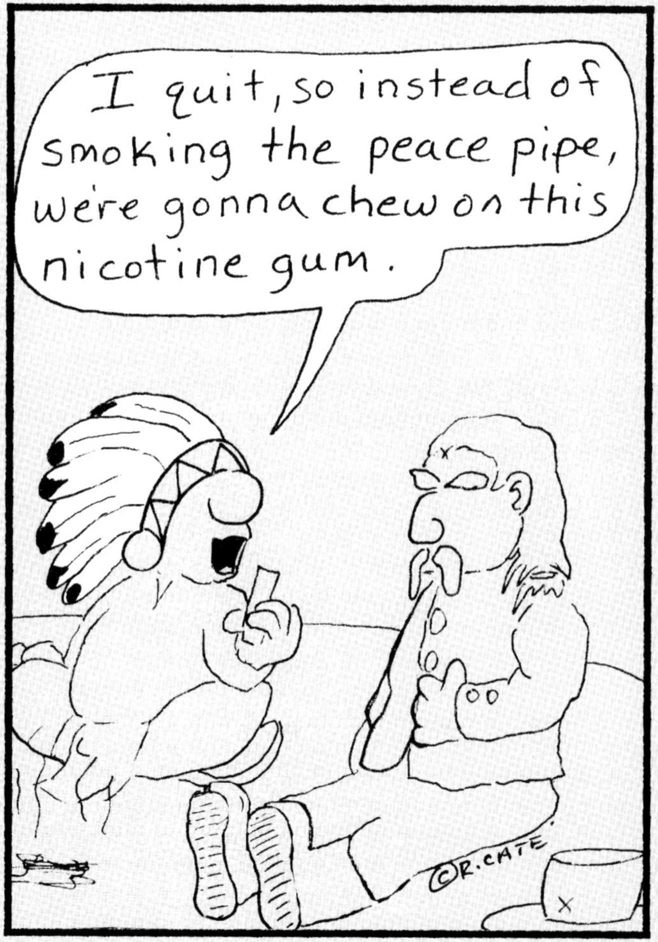
I quit, so instead of smoking the peace pipe, we're gonna chew on this nicotine gum.
©R.CATE

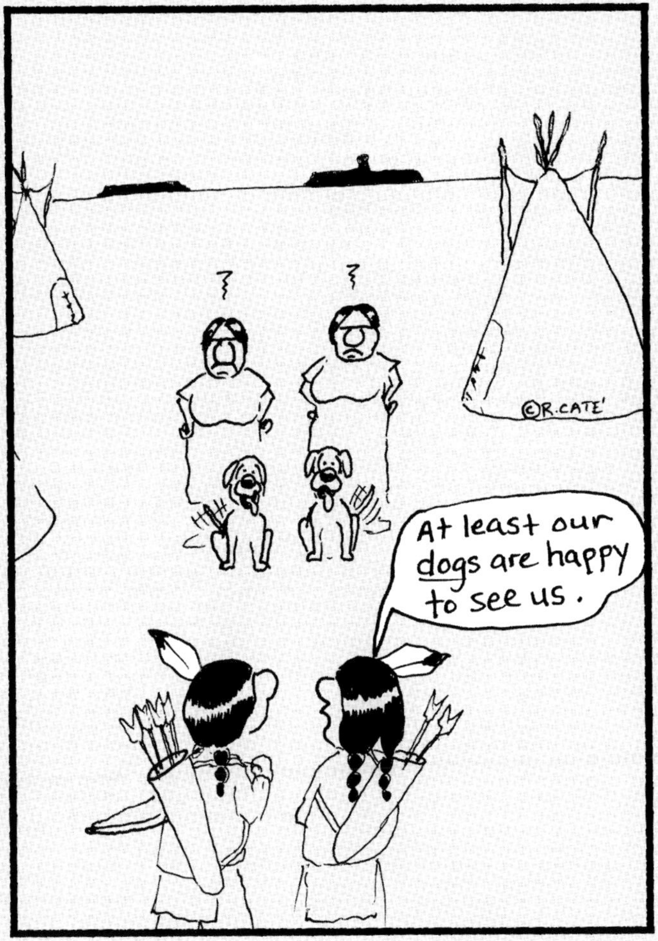
©R.CATE'
At least our dogs are happy to see us.

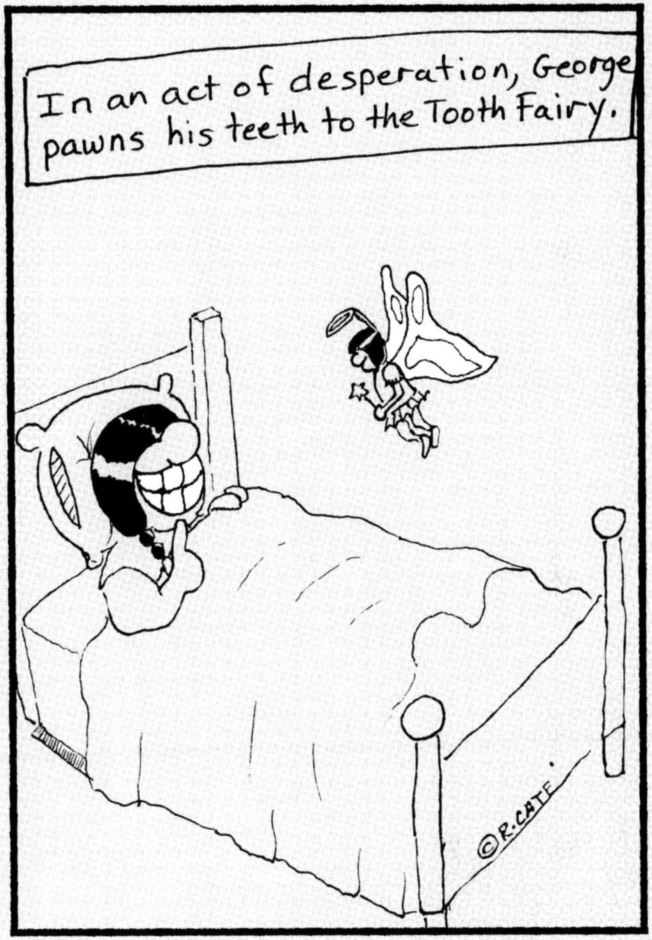
In an act of desperation, George pawns his teeth to the Tooth Fairy.
©R.CATE'

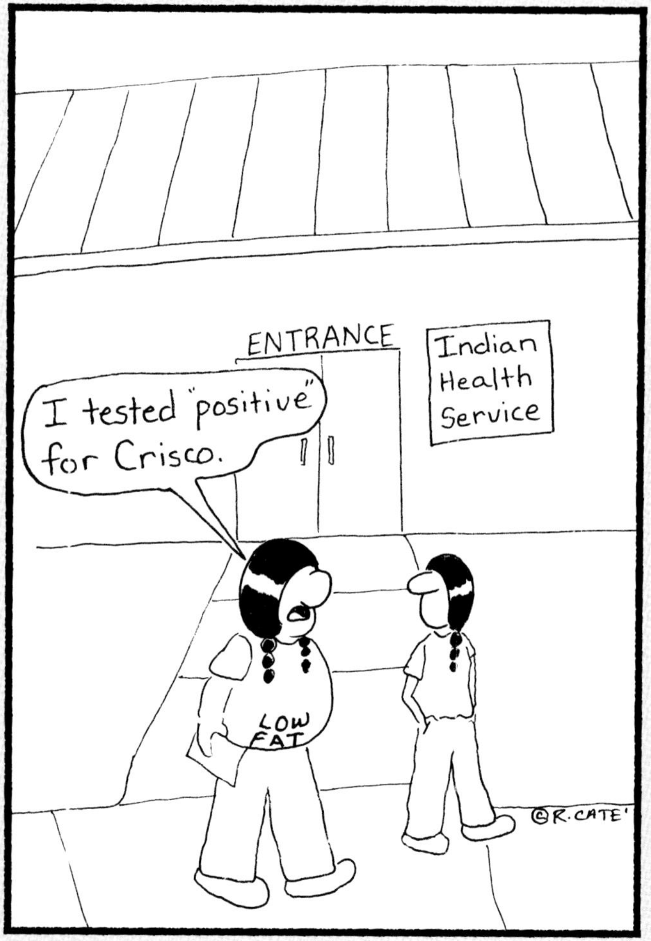
ENTRANCE
Indian Health Service
I tested "positive" for Crisco.
LOW FAT
©R. CATE'

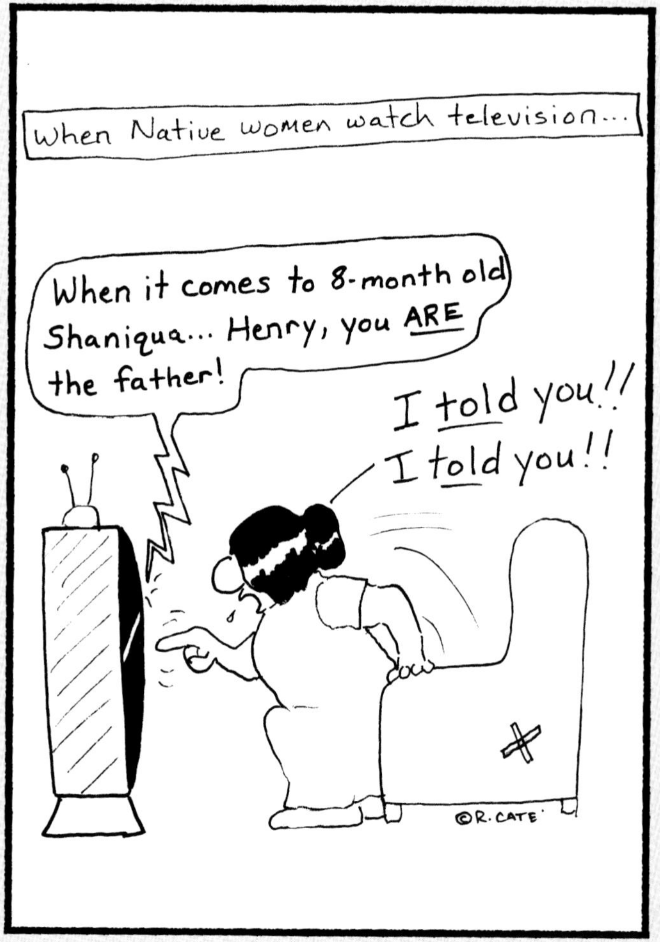
When Native women watch television...
When it comes to 8-month old Shaniqua... Henry, you ARE the father!
I told you!! I told you!!
©R. CATE'

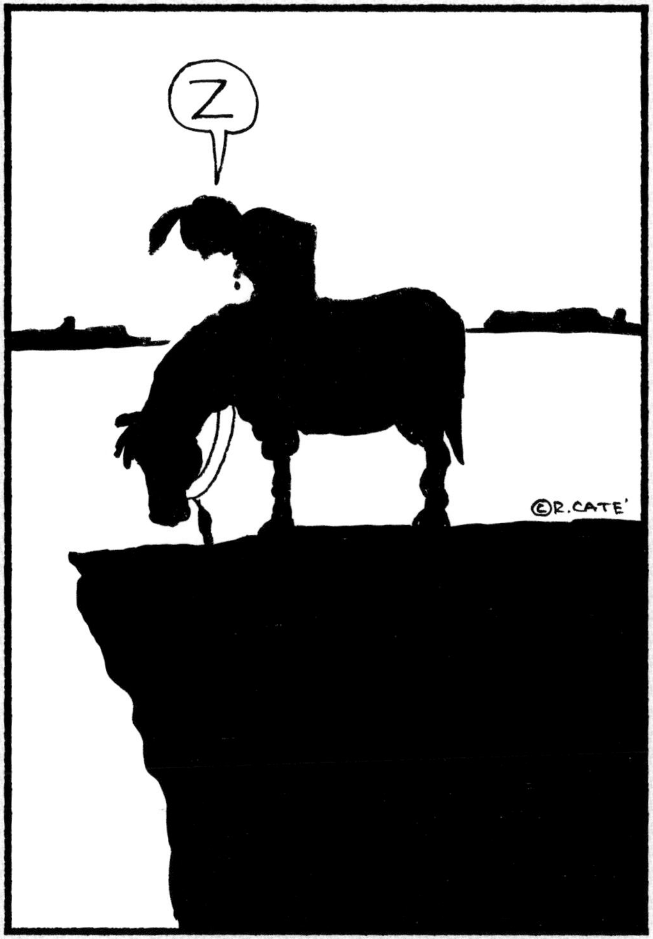
Z
©R. CATE'

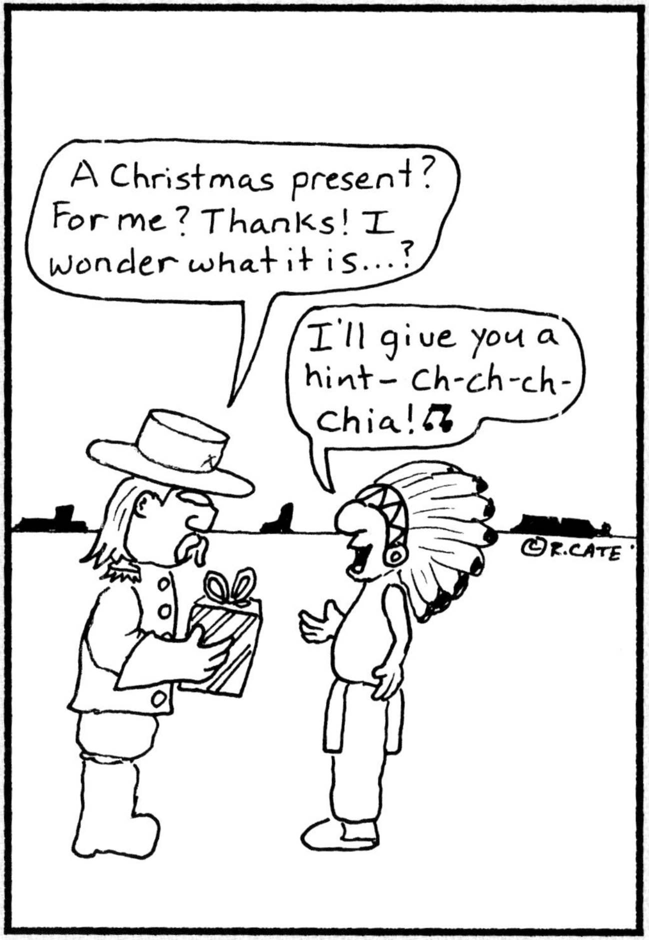
A Christmas present? For me? Thanks! I wonder what it is...?
I'll give you a hint– Ch-ch-ch-Chia!
©R. CATE'

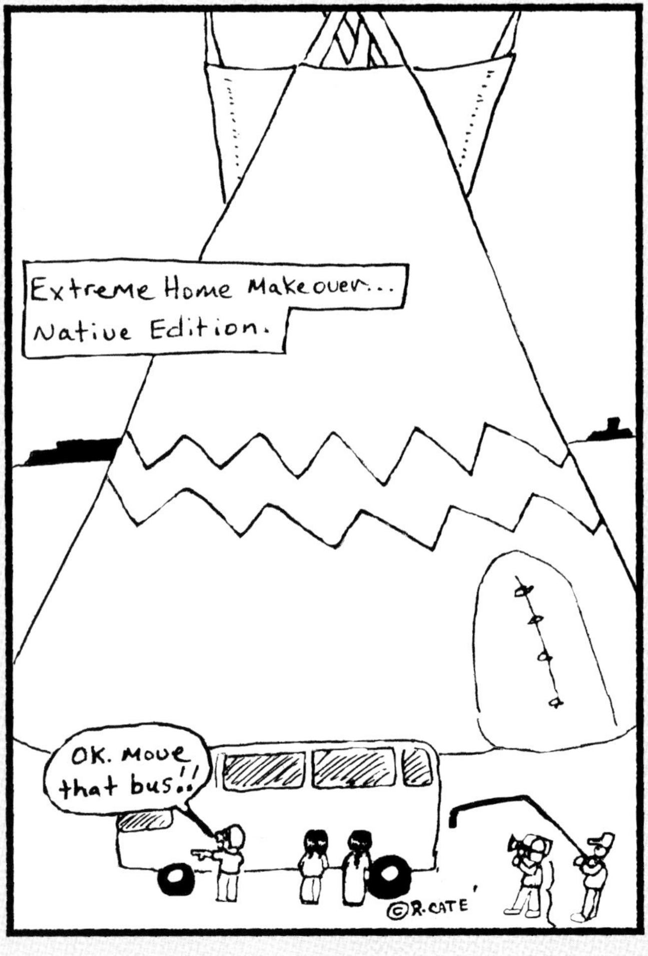
Extreme Home Makeover...
Native Edition.
OK. Move that bus!!
©R.CATE'

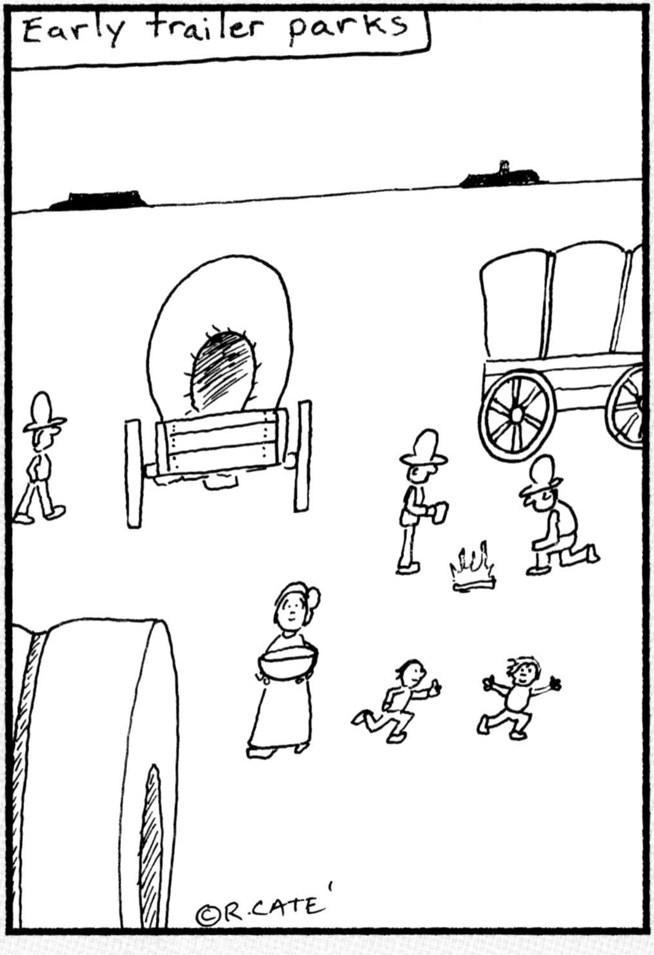
Early trailer parks
©R.CATE'

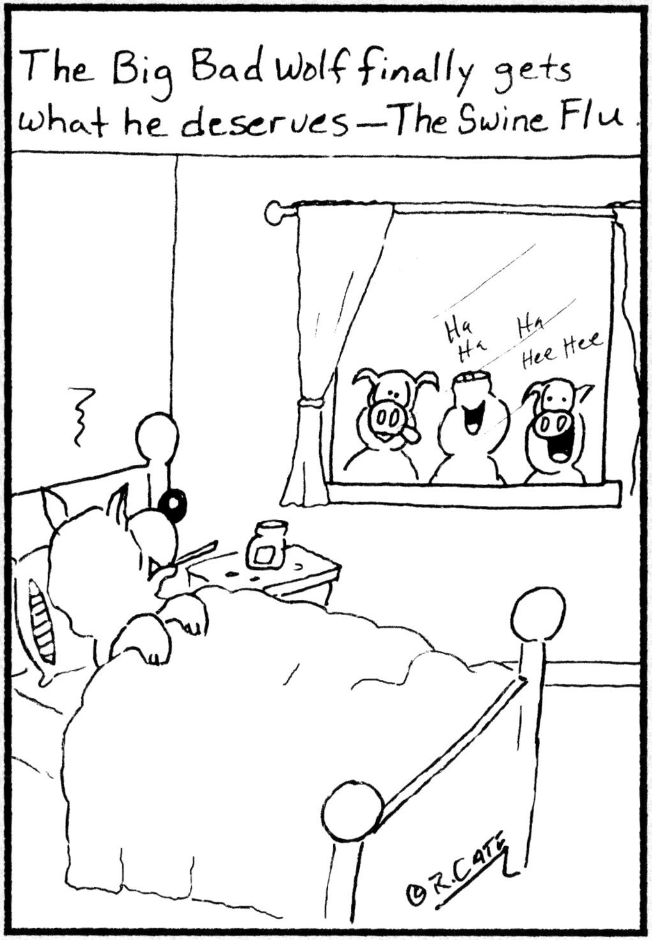
The Big Bad Wolf finally gets what he deserves—The Swine Flu.
Ha Ha
Ha
Hee Hee
©R.CATE

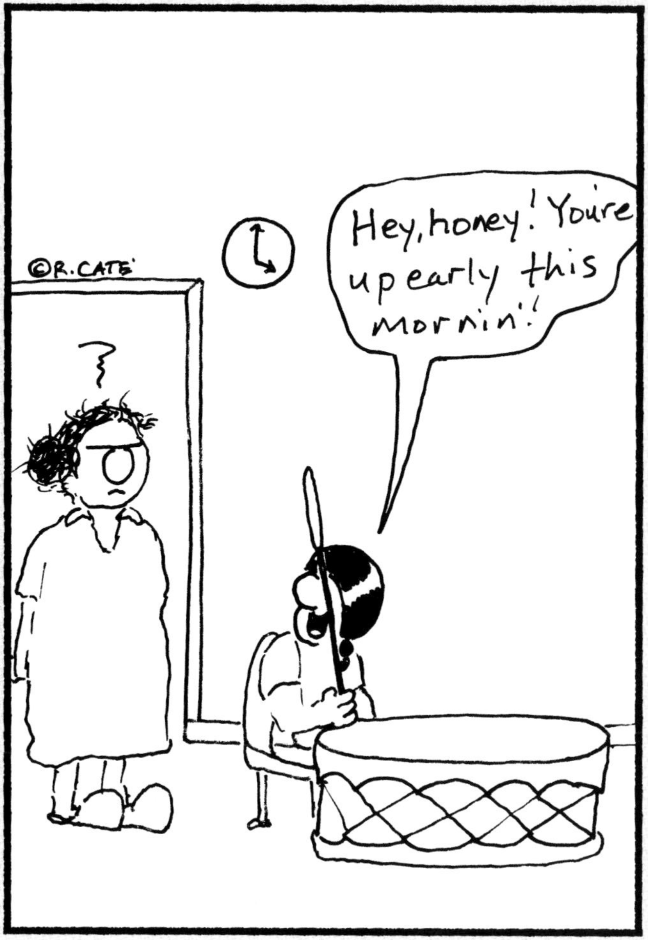
©R.CATE
Hey, honey! You're up early this mornin'!

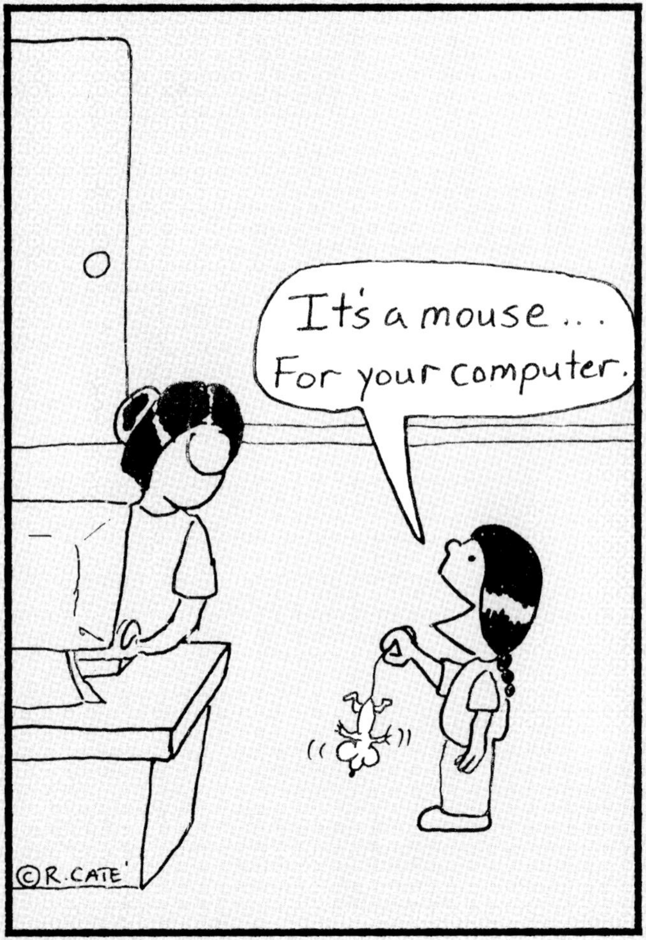

It's a mouse...
For your computer.
©R. CATE'

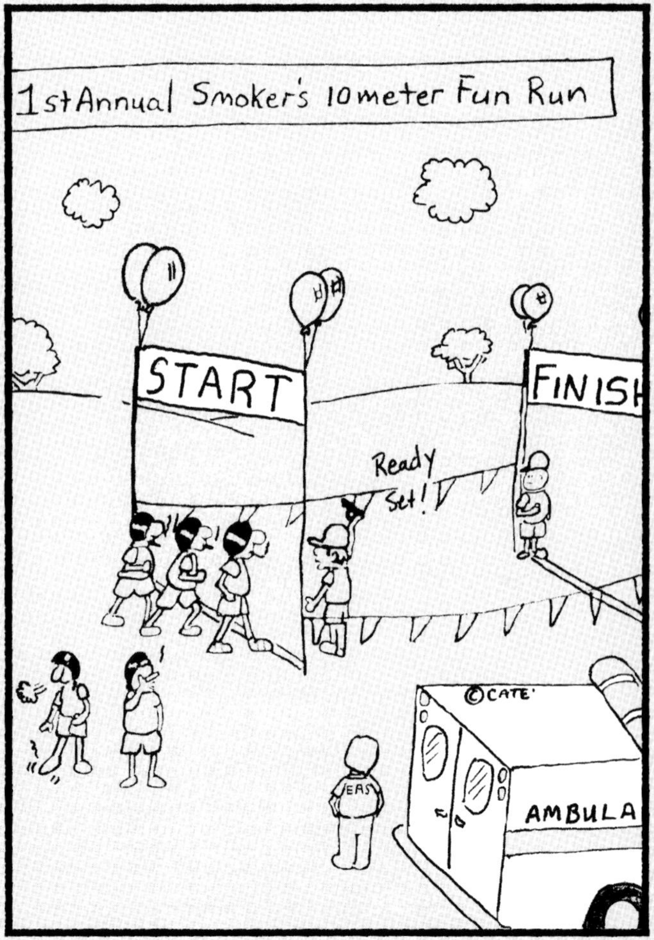

1st Annual Smoker's 10 meter Fun Run
START
FINISH
Ready
Set!
EAS
AMBULA
©CATE'

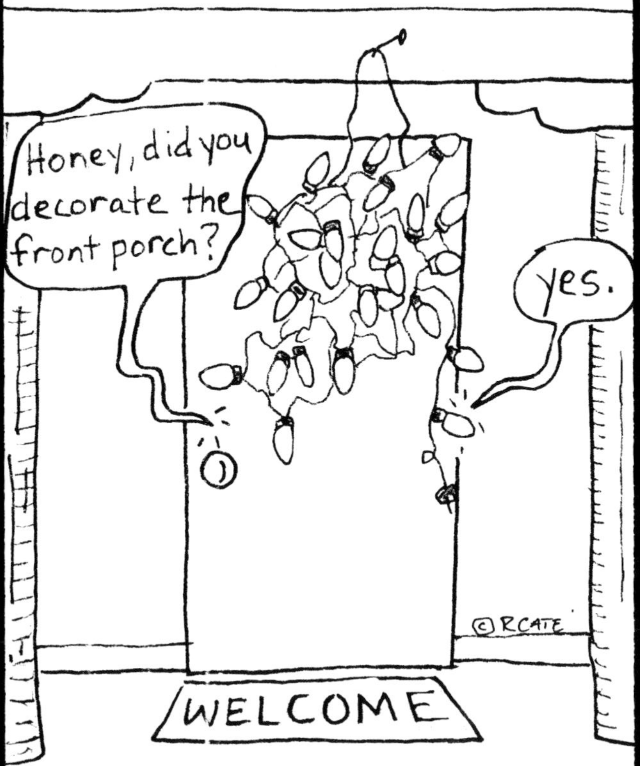
Honey, did you decorate the front porch?
yes.
WELCOME
©RCATE

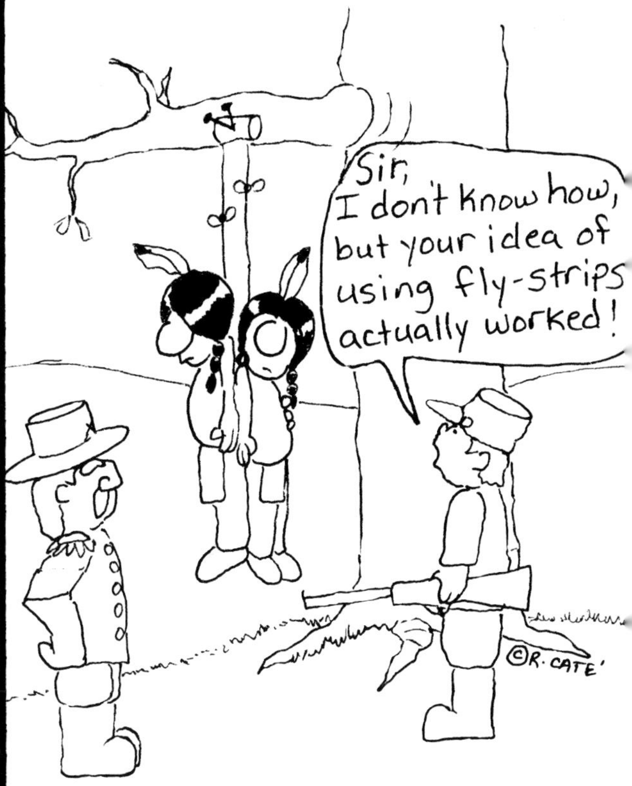
Sir, I don't know how, but your idea of using fly-strips actually worked!
©R. CATE

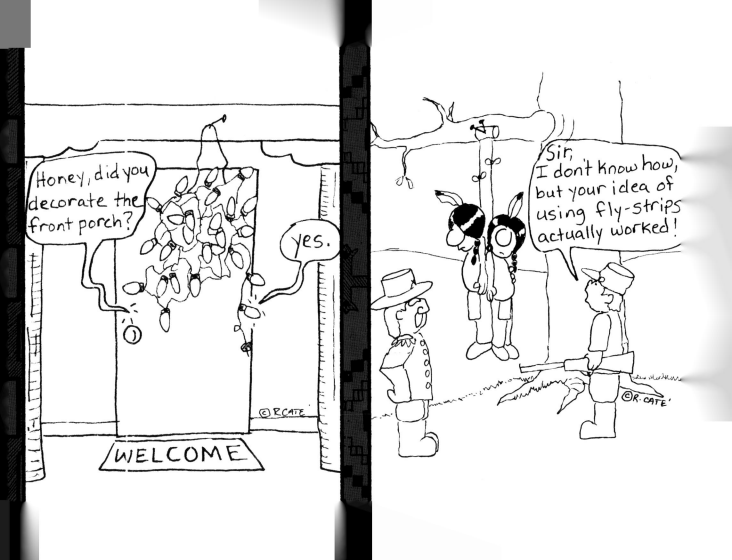

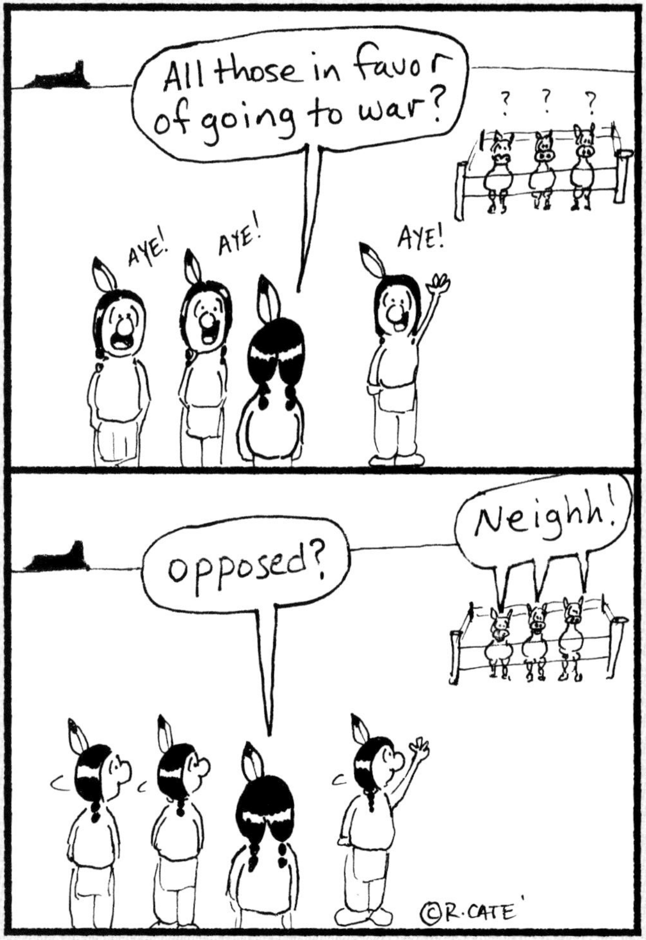
All those in favor of going to war?
? ? ?
AYE!
AYE!
AYE!
Opposed?
Neighh!
©R.CATE

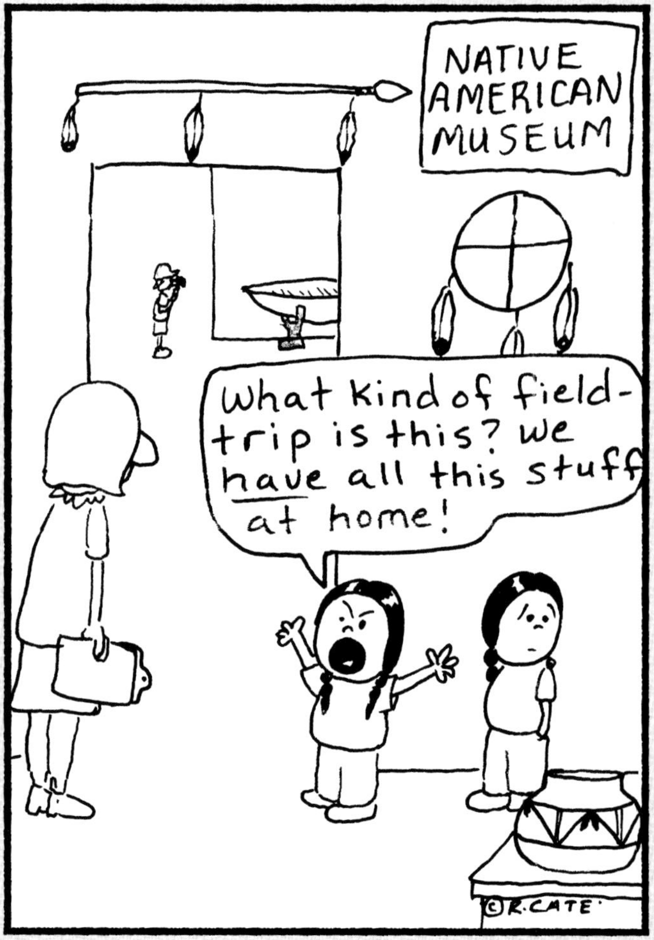
NATIVE AMERICAN MUSEUM
What kind of field-trip is this? we have all this stuff at home!
©R.CATE

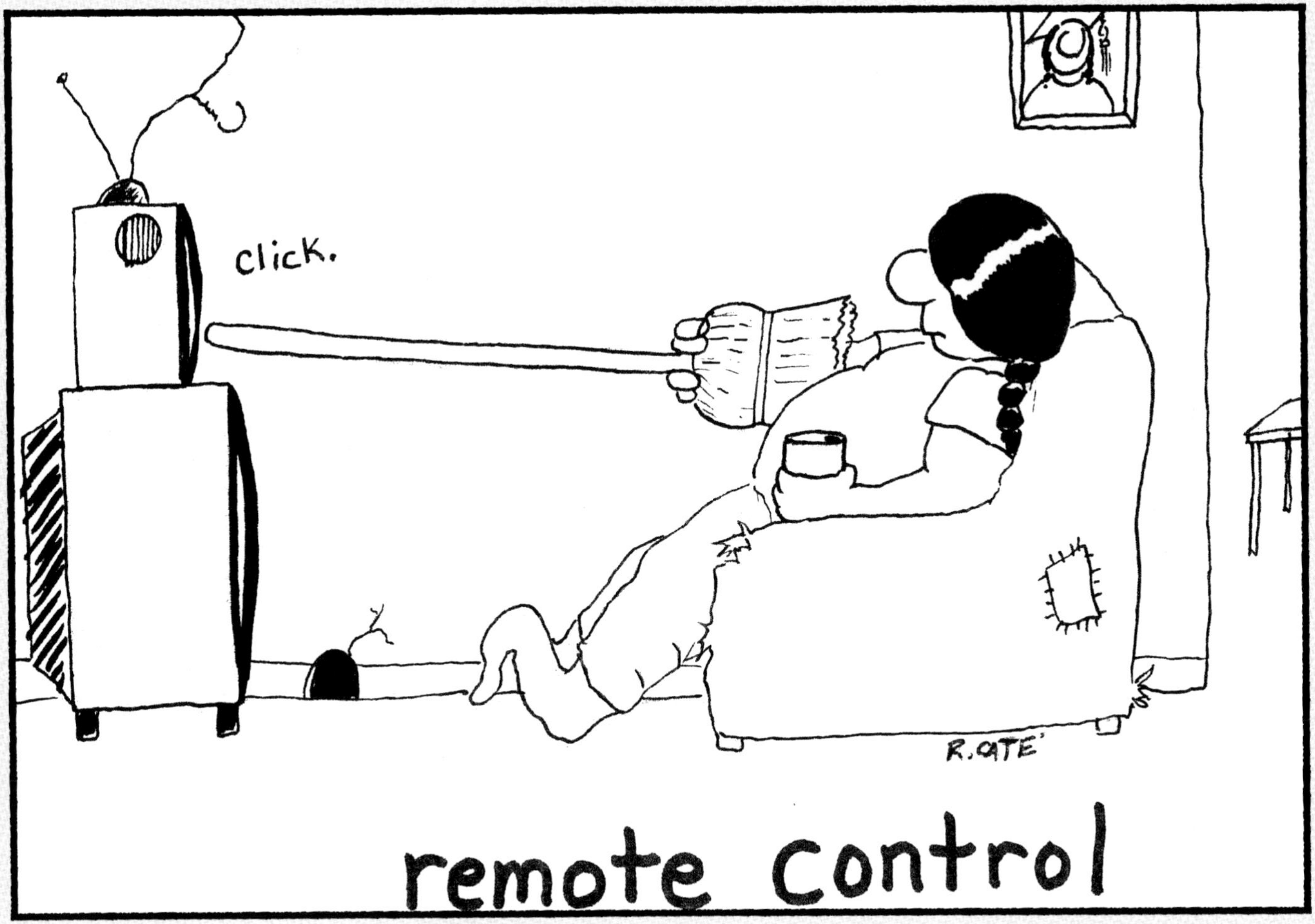
click.
R.CATE'

remote control

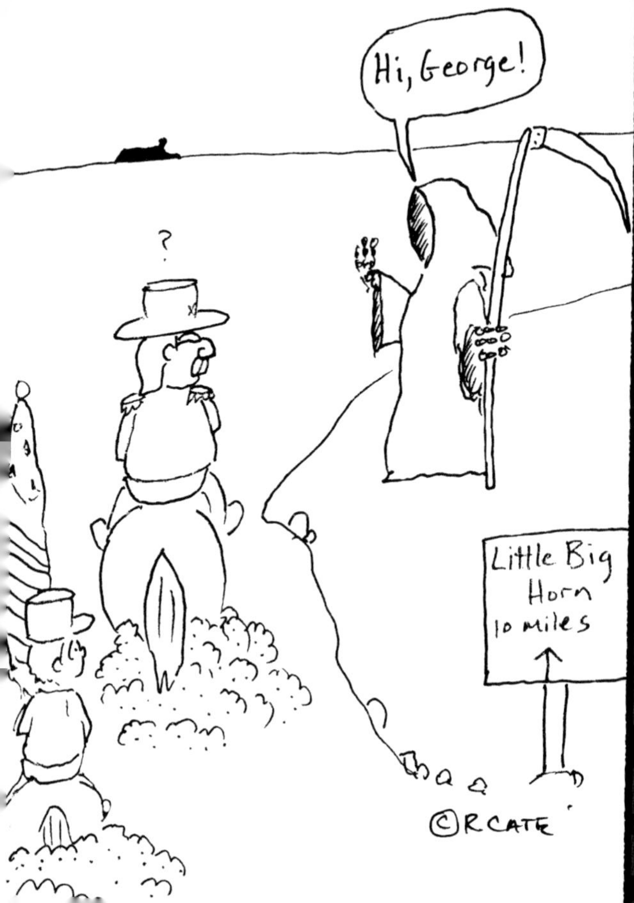
Hi, George!
Little Big Horn 10 miles
©RCATE

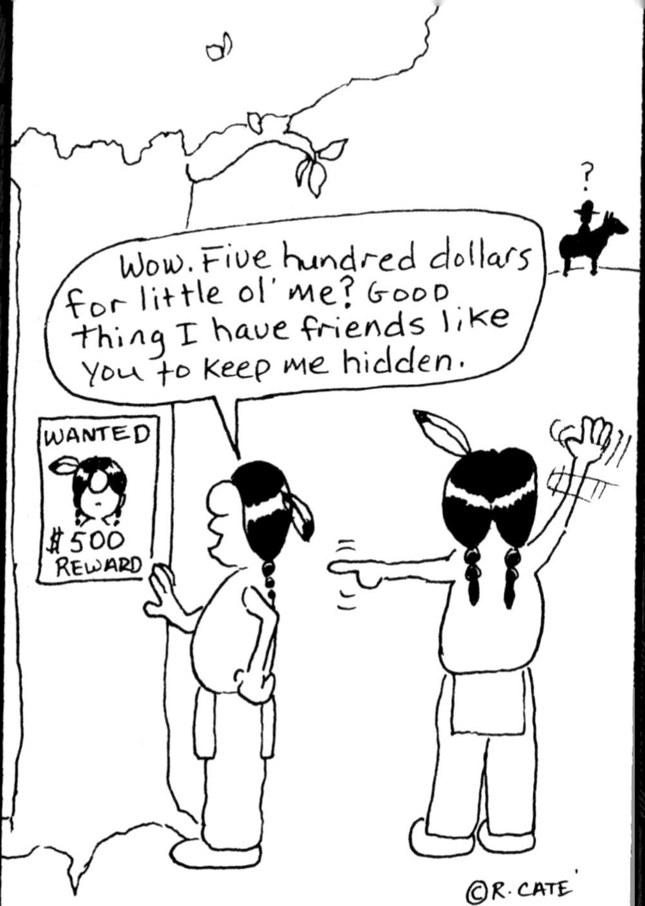
Wow. Five hundred dollars for little ol' me? Good thing I have friends like you to keep me hidden.
WANTED
$500 REWARD
©R. CATE

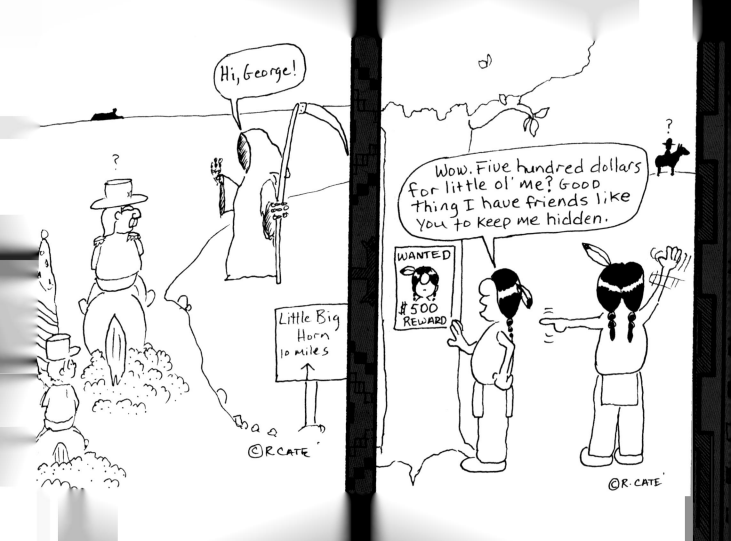

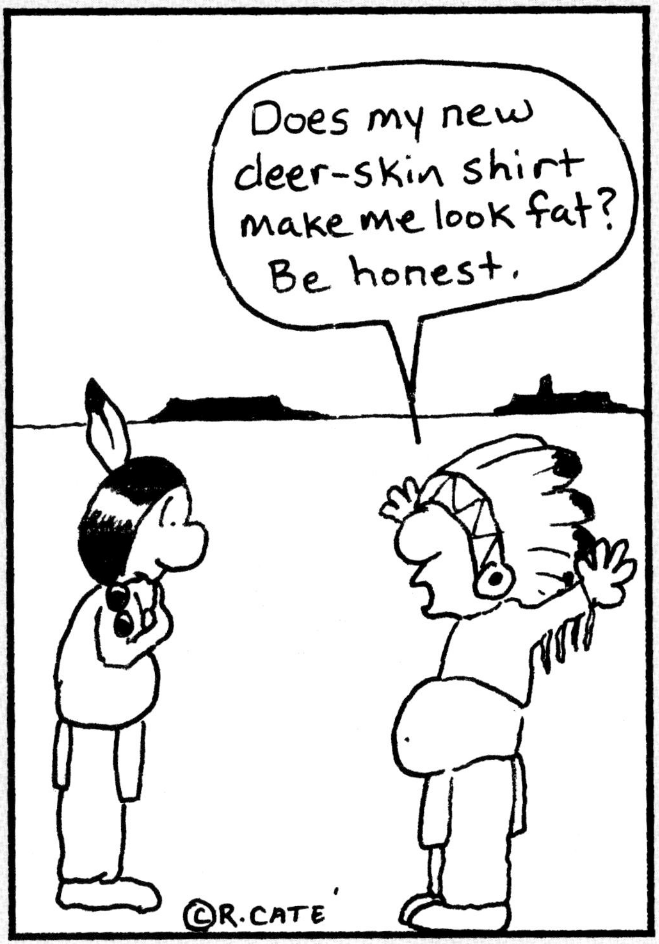
Does my new deer-skin shirt make me look fat? Be honest.
©R.CATE'

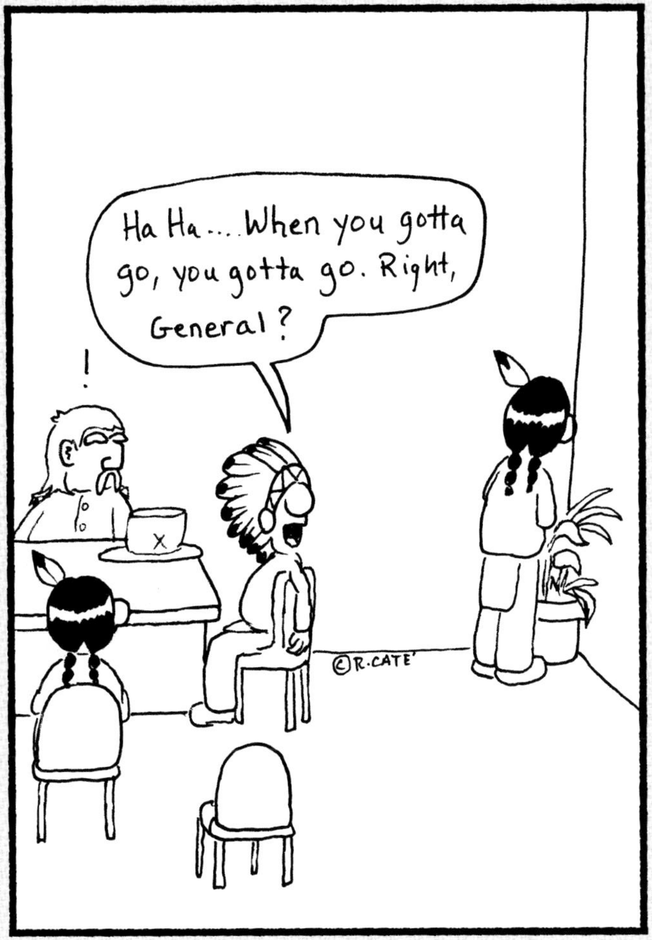
Ha Ha.... When you gotta go, you gotta go. Right, General?
!
©R.CATE'

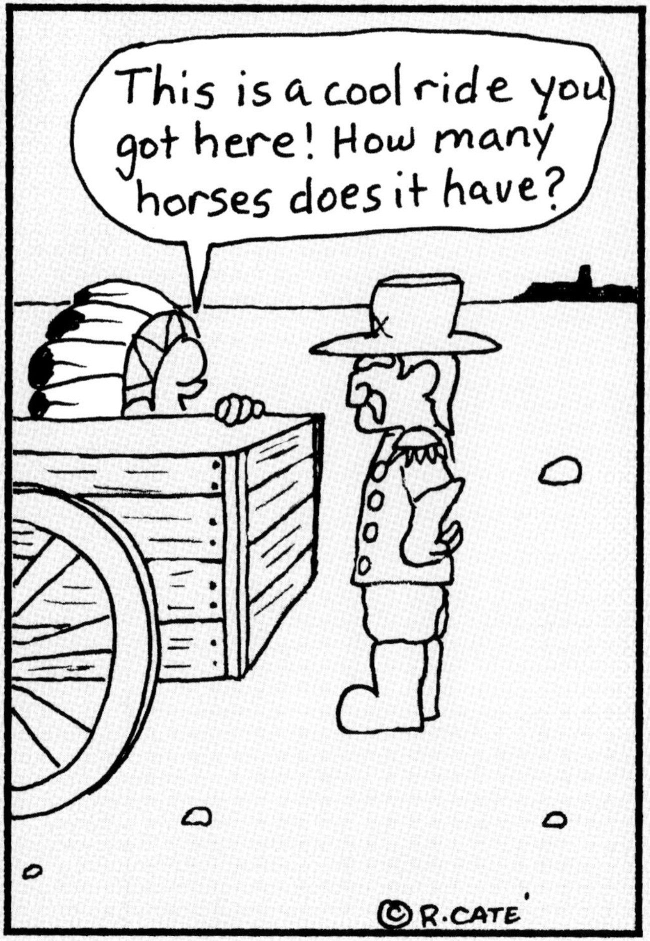
This is a cool ride you got here! How many horses does it have?
© R. CATE

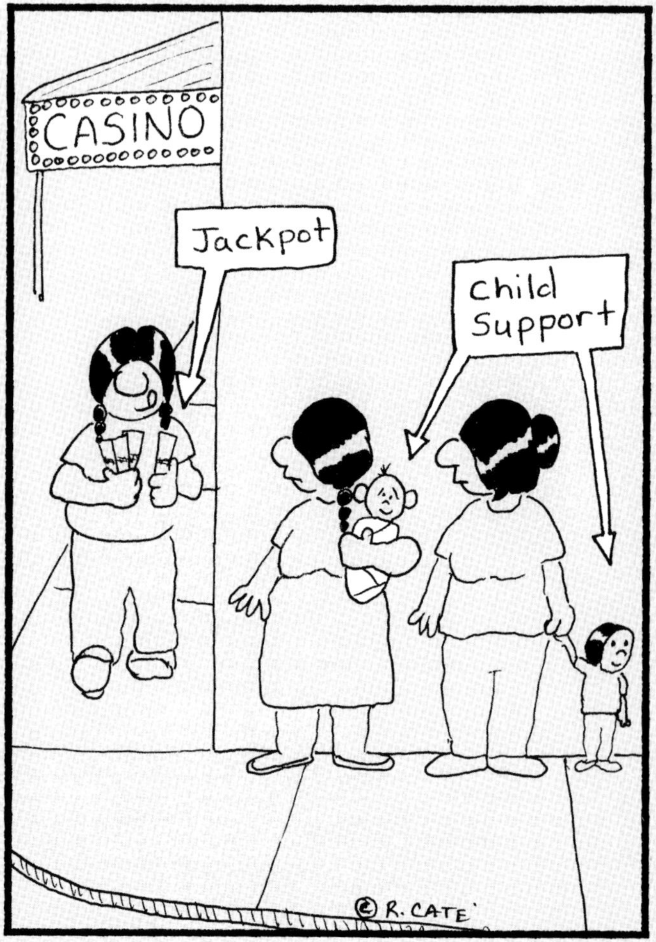
CASINO
Jackpot
Child Support
© R. CATE

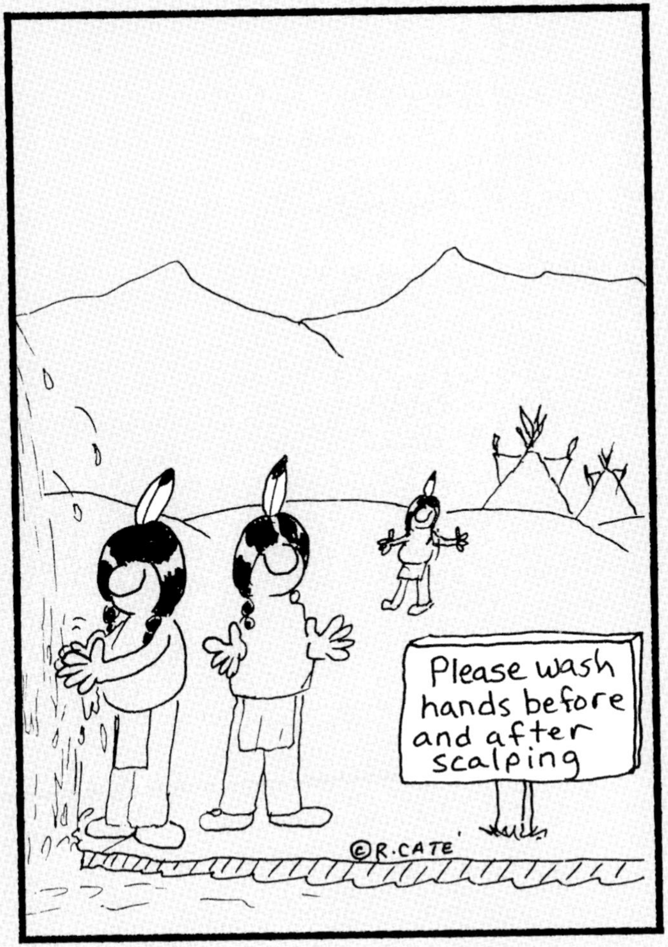
Please wash hands before and after scalping
©R. CATE

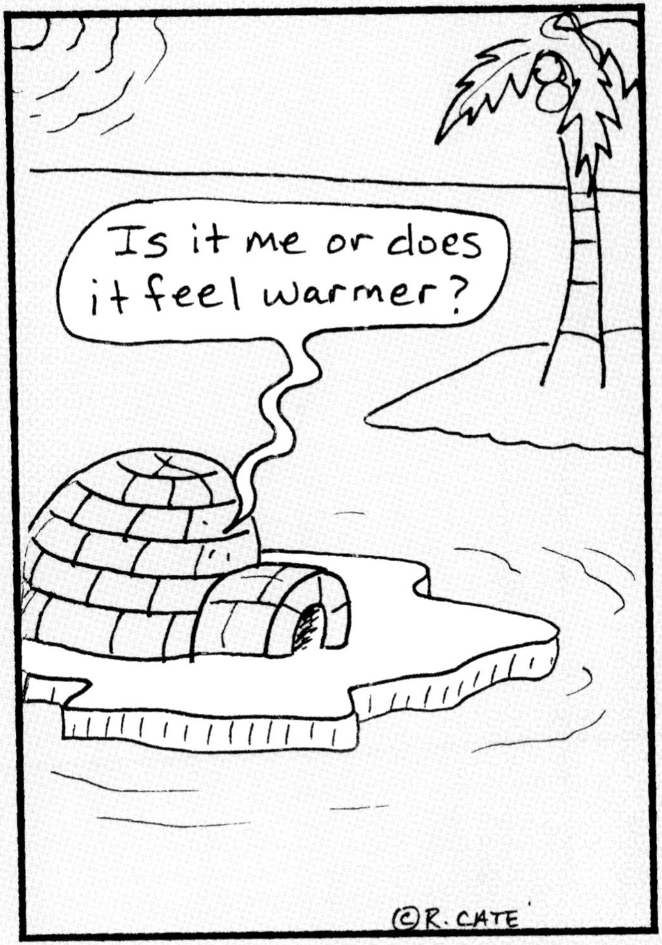
Is it me or does it feel warmer?
©R. CATE

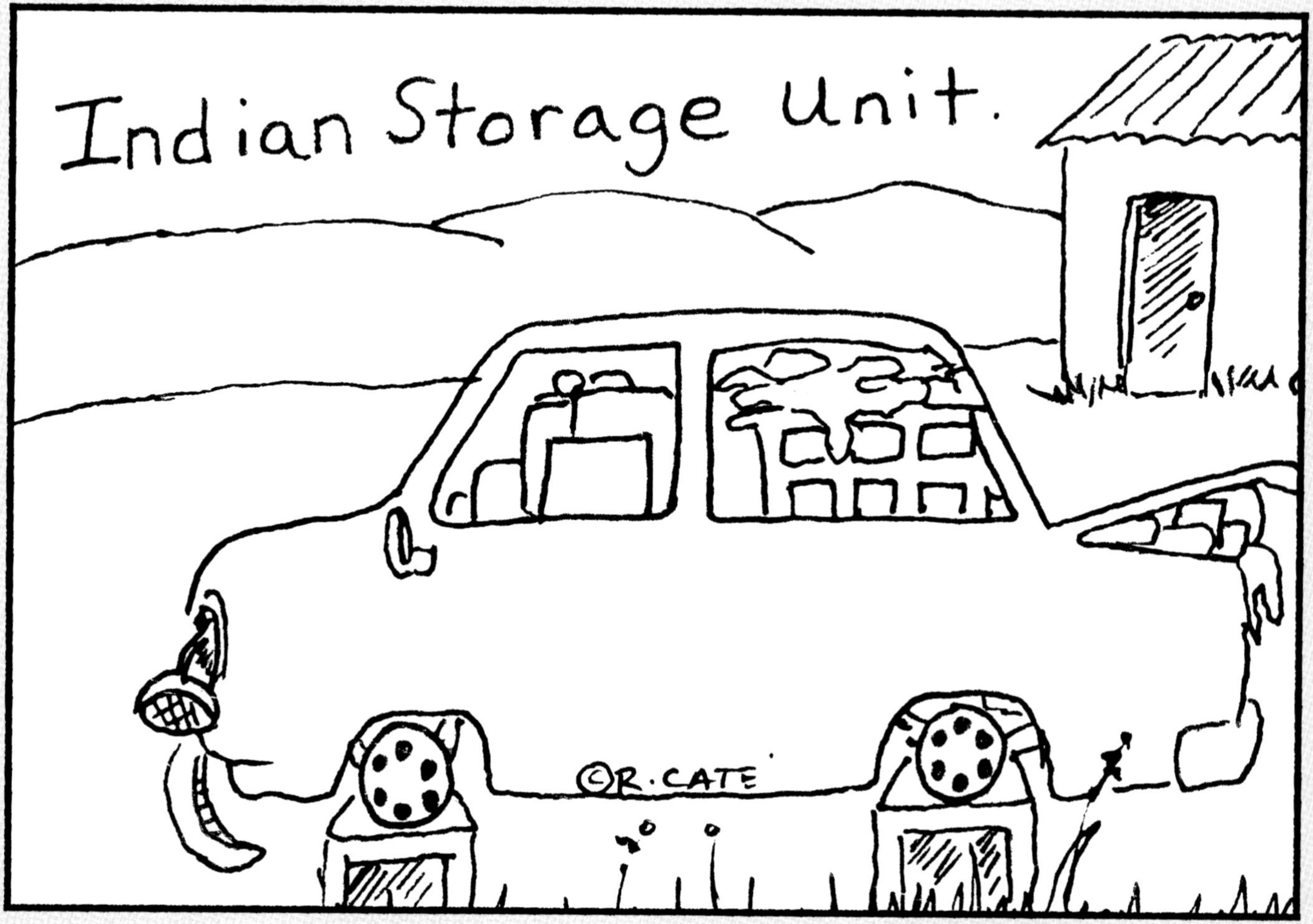
Indian Storage Unit.
©R. CATE

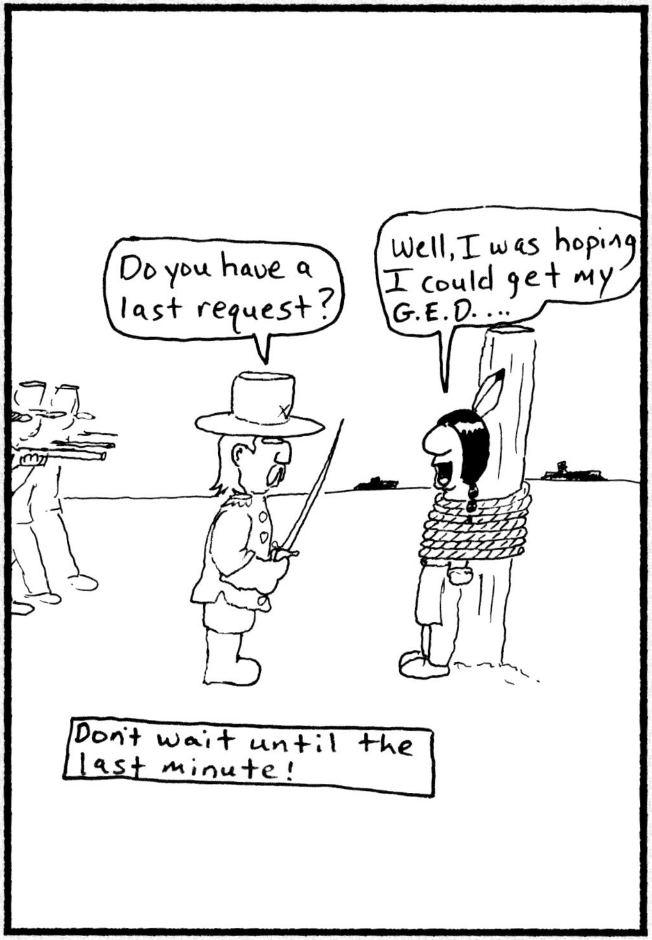
Do you have a last request?
Well, I was hoping I could get my G.E.D. ...
Don't wait until the last minute!

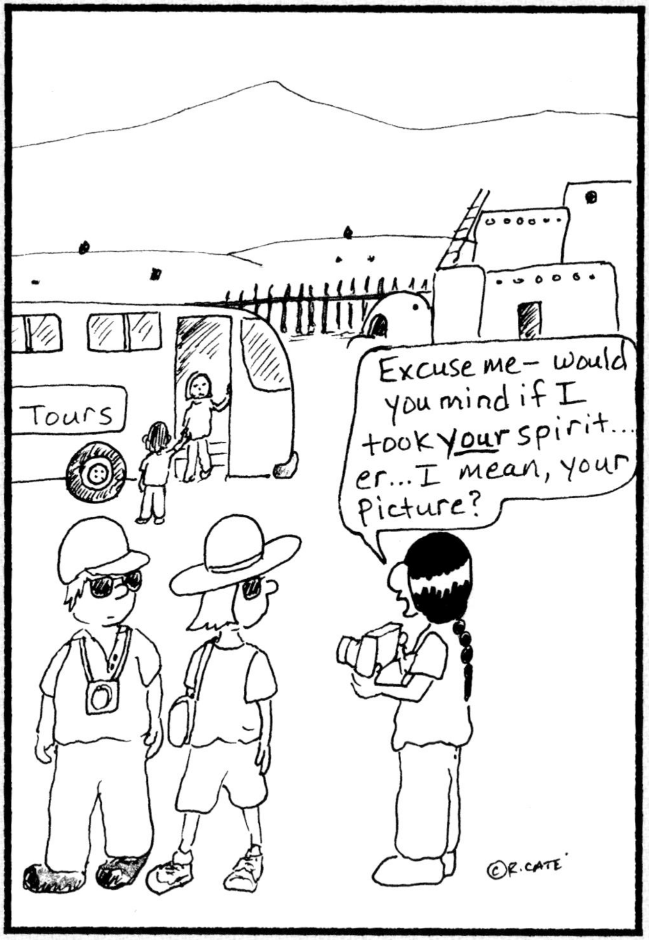
Tours
Excuse me– would you mind if I took your spirit... er... I mean, your picture?
©R.CATE

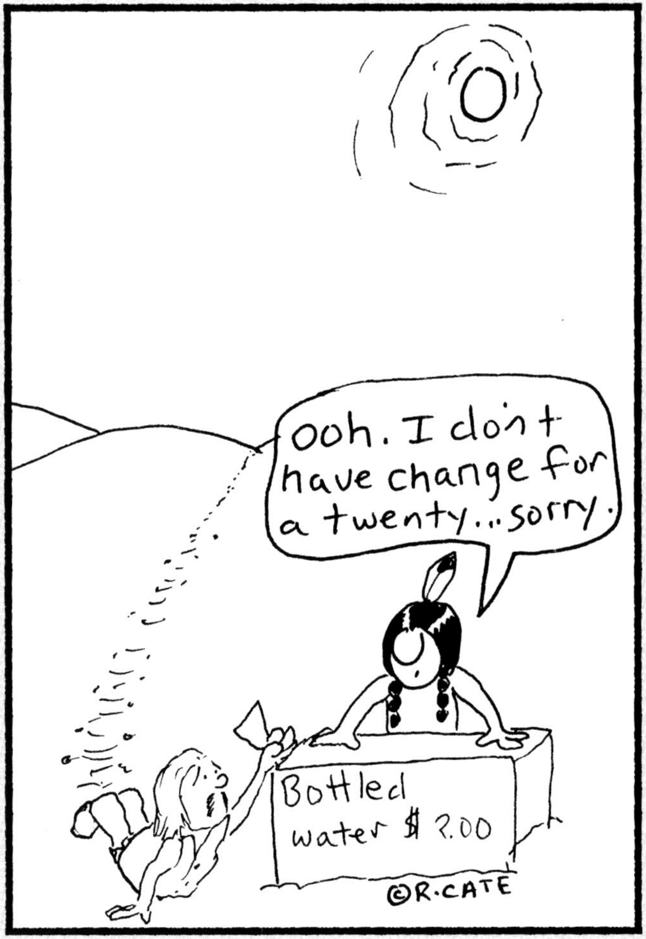
Ooh. I don't have change for a twenty...sorry.
Bottled water $ 2.00
©R.CATE

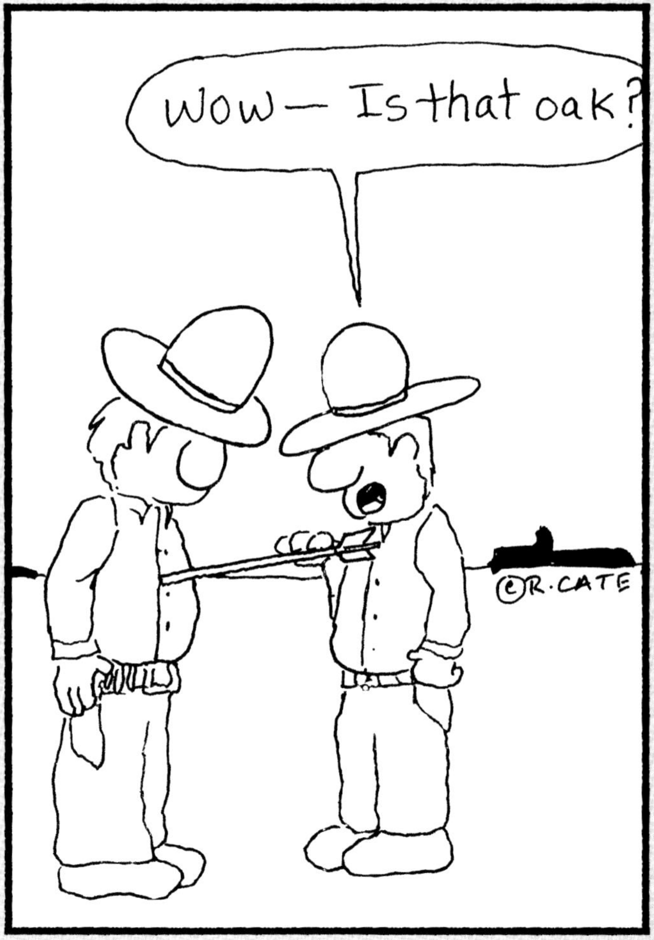
Wow— Is that oak?
©R.CATE

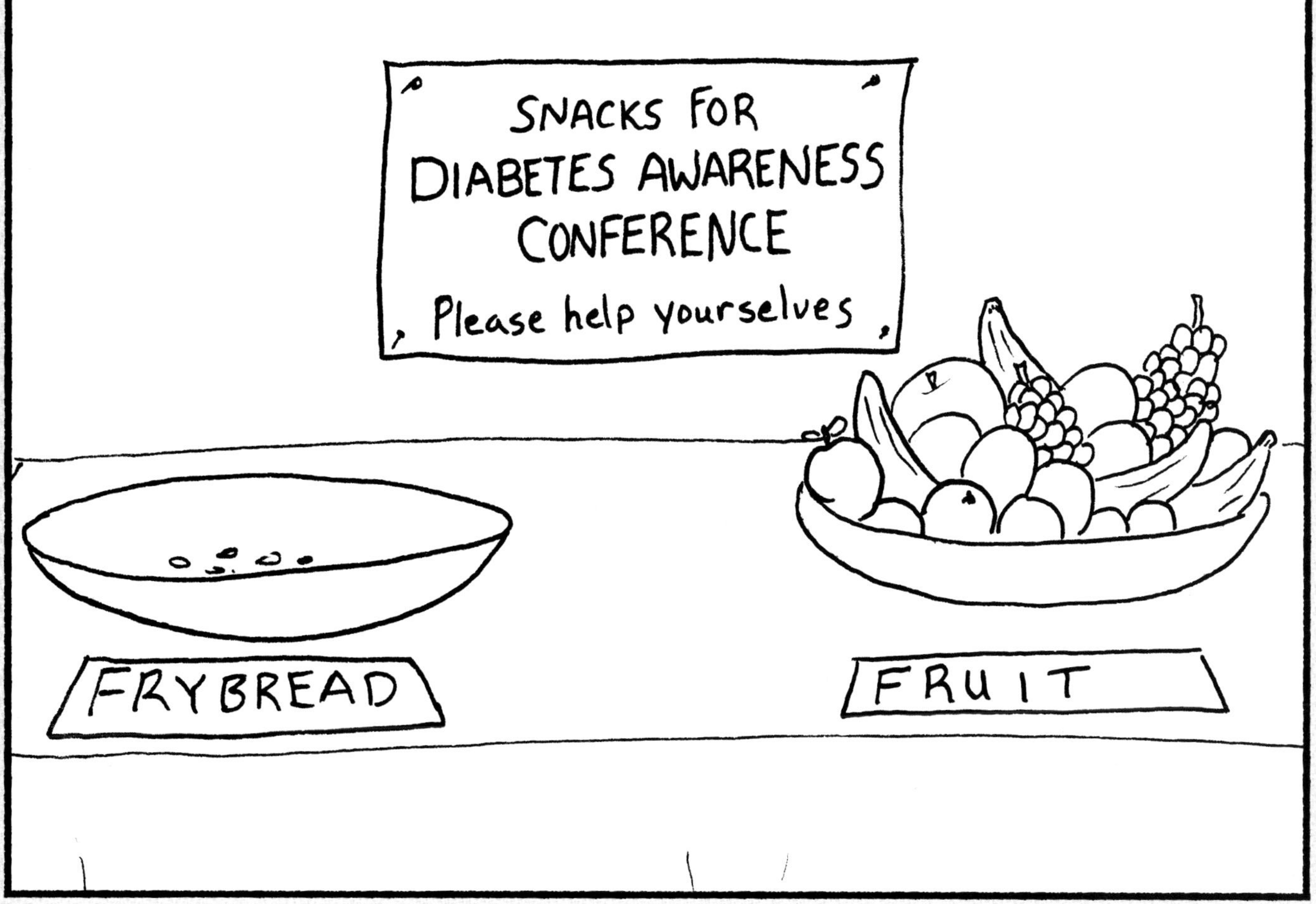
SNACKS FOR
DIABETES AWARENESS
CONFERENCE
Please help yourselves
FRYBREAD
FRUIT

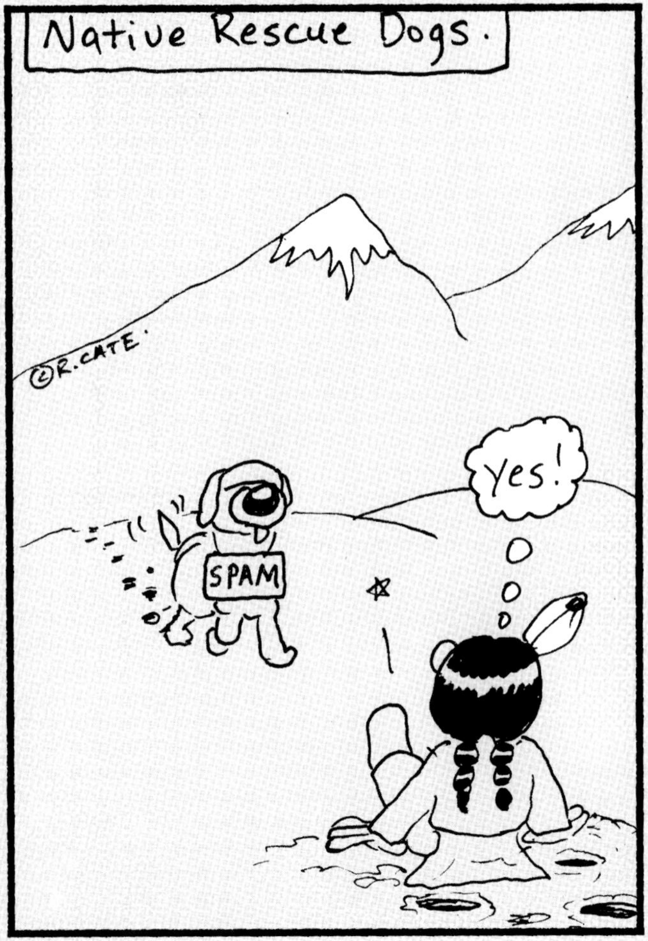
Native Rescue Dogs.
SPAM
Yes!
©R.CATE.

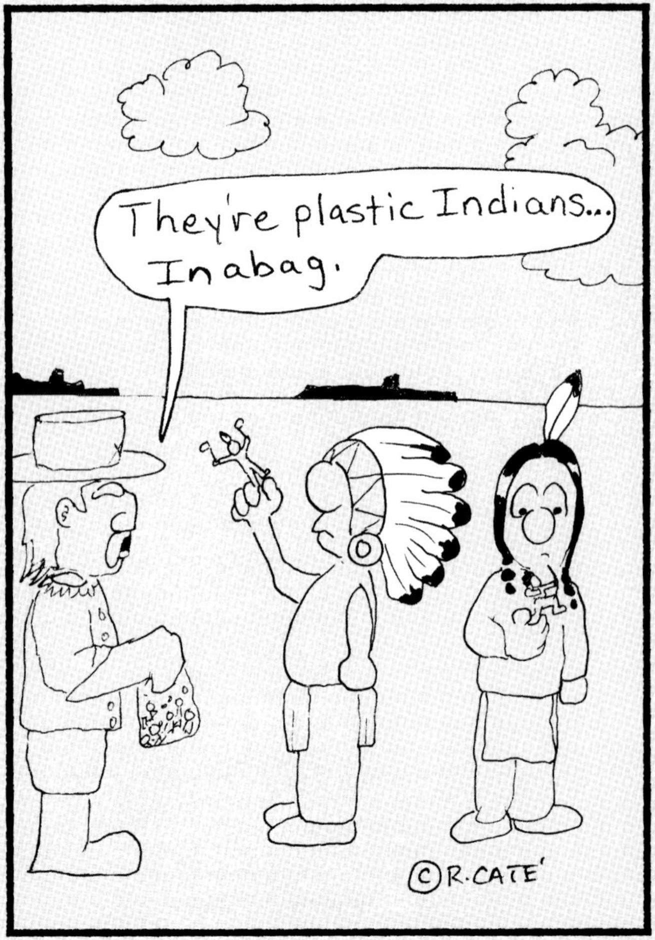
They're plastic Indians...
In a bag.
©R.CATE'

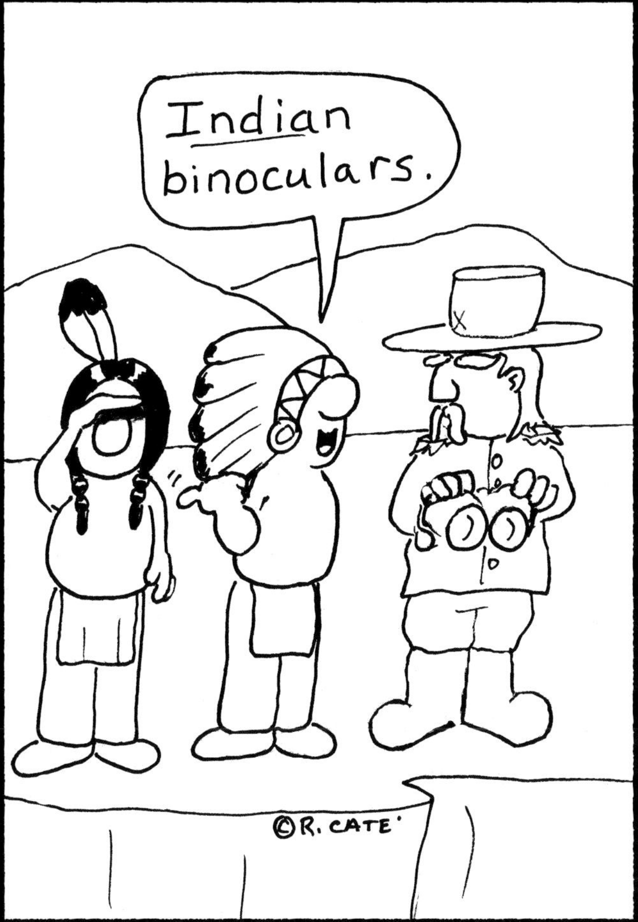
Indian binoculars.
©R. CATE

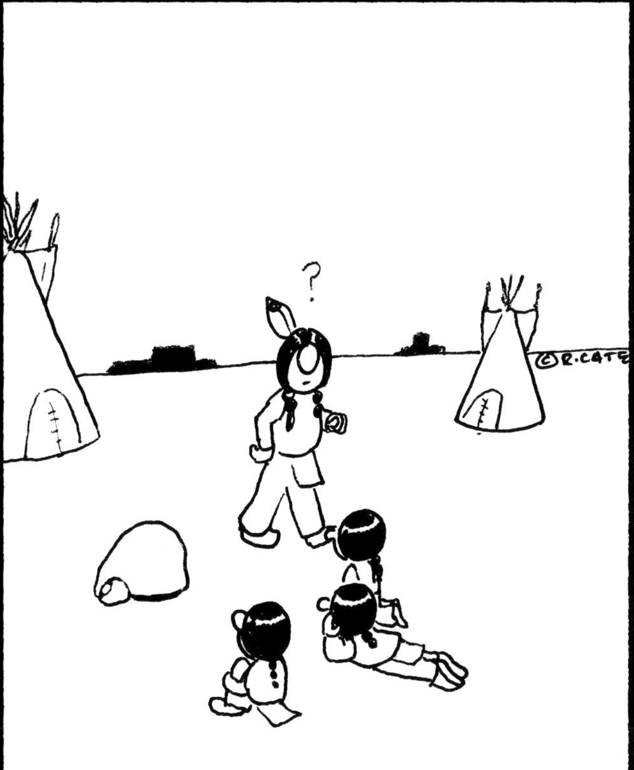
?
©R. CATE

Before television

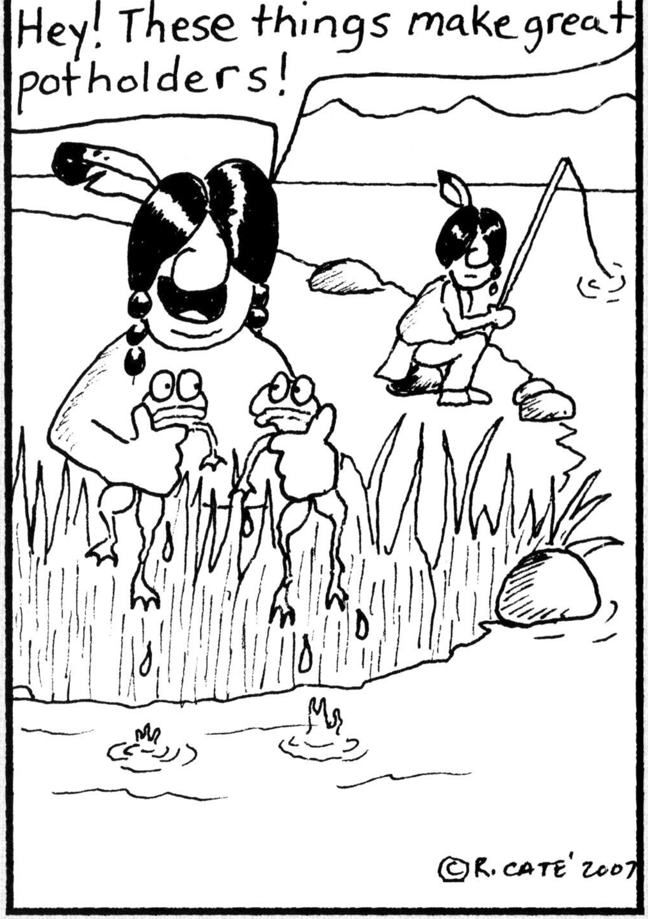
Hey! These things make great potholders!
©R. CATE' 2007

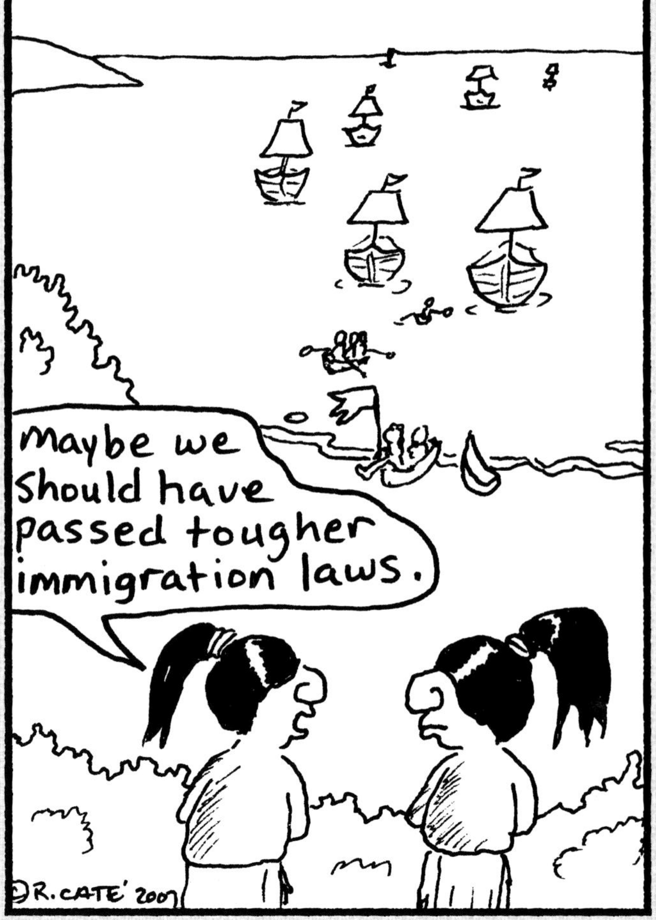
Maybe we should have passed tougher immigration laws.
©R. CATE' 2007

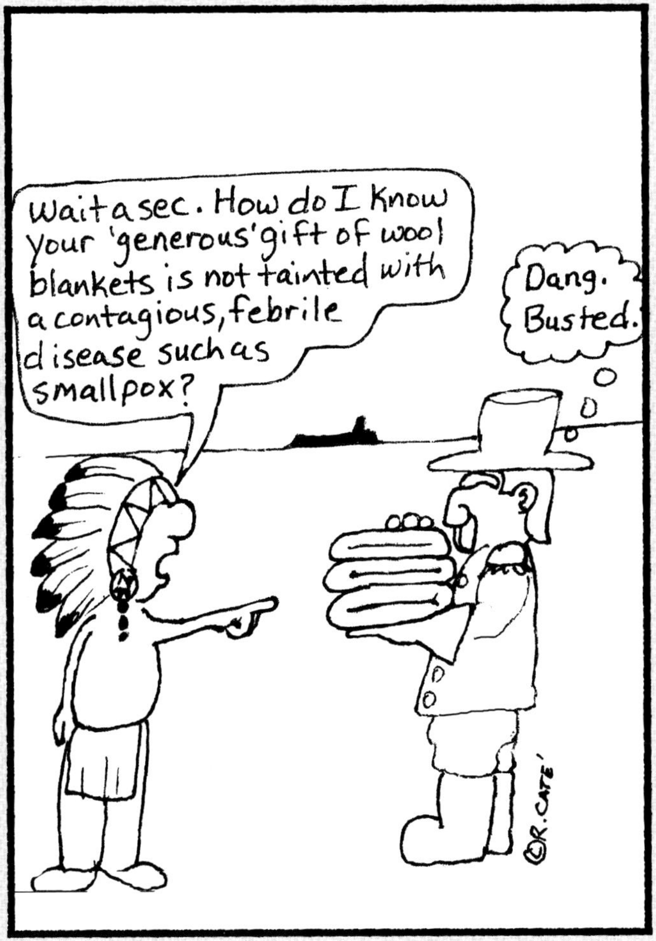
Wait a sec. How do I know your 'generous' gift of wool blankets is not tainted with a contagious, febrile disease such as smallpox?
Dang. Busted.
©R. CATE'

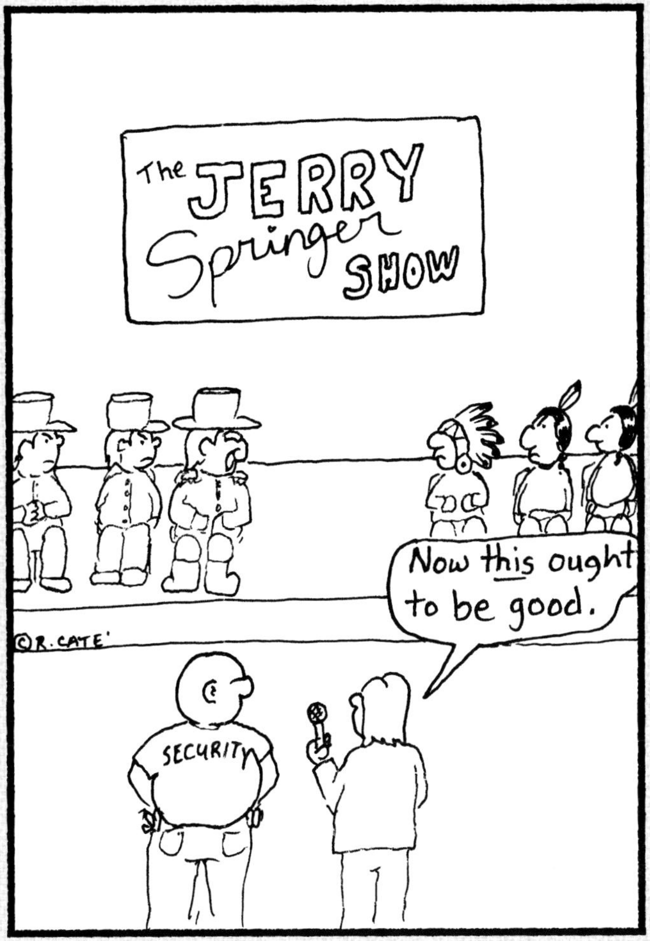
The JERRY Springer SHOW
Now this ought to be good.
SECURITY
©R. CATE'

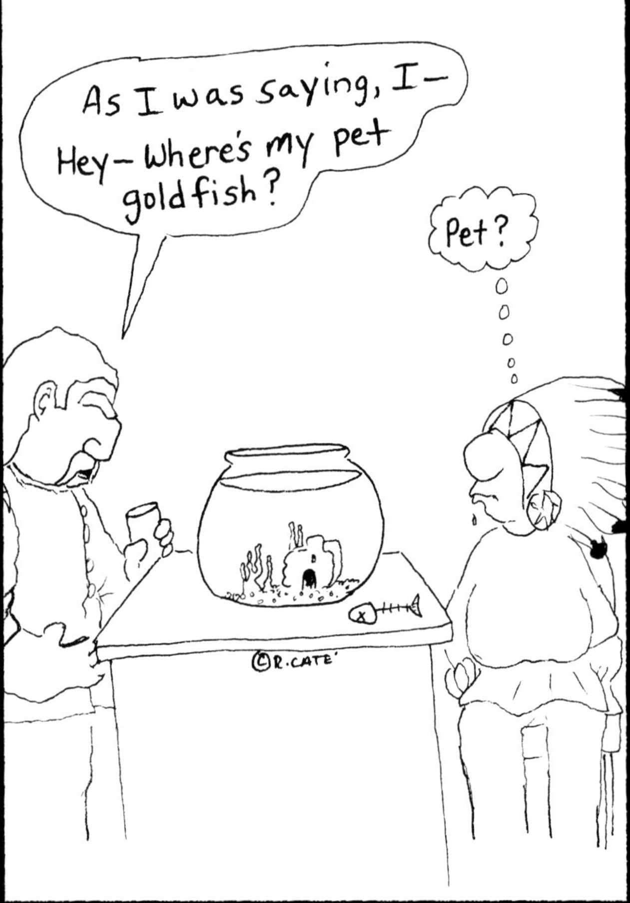
As I was saying, I— Hey—Where's my pet goldfish?
Pet?
©R. CATE'

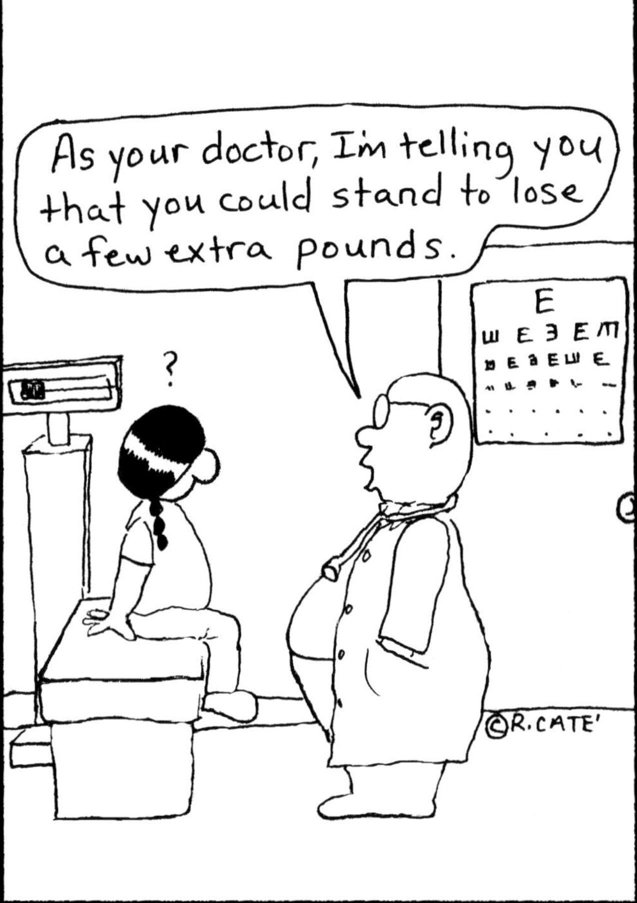
As your doctor, I'm telling you that you could stand to lose a few extra pounds.
?
©R. CATE'

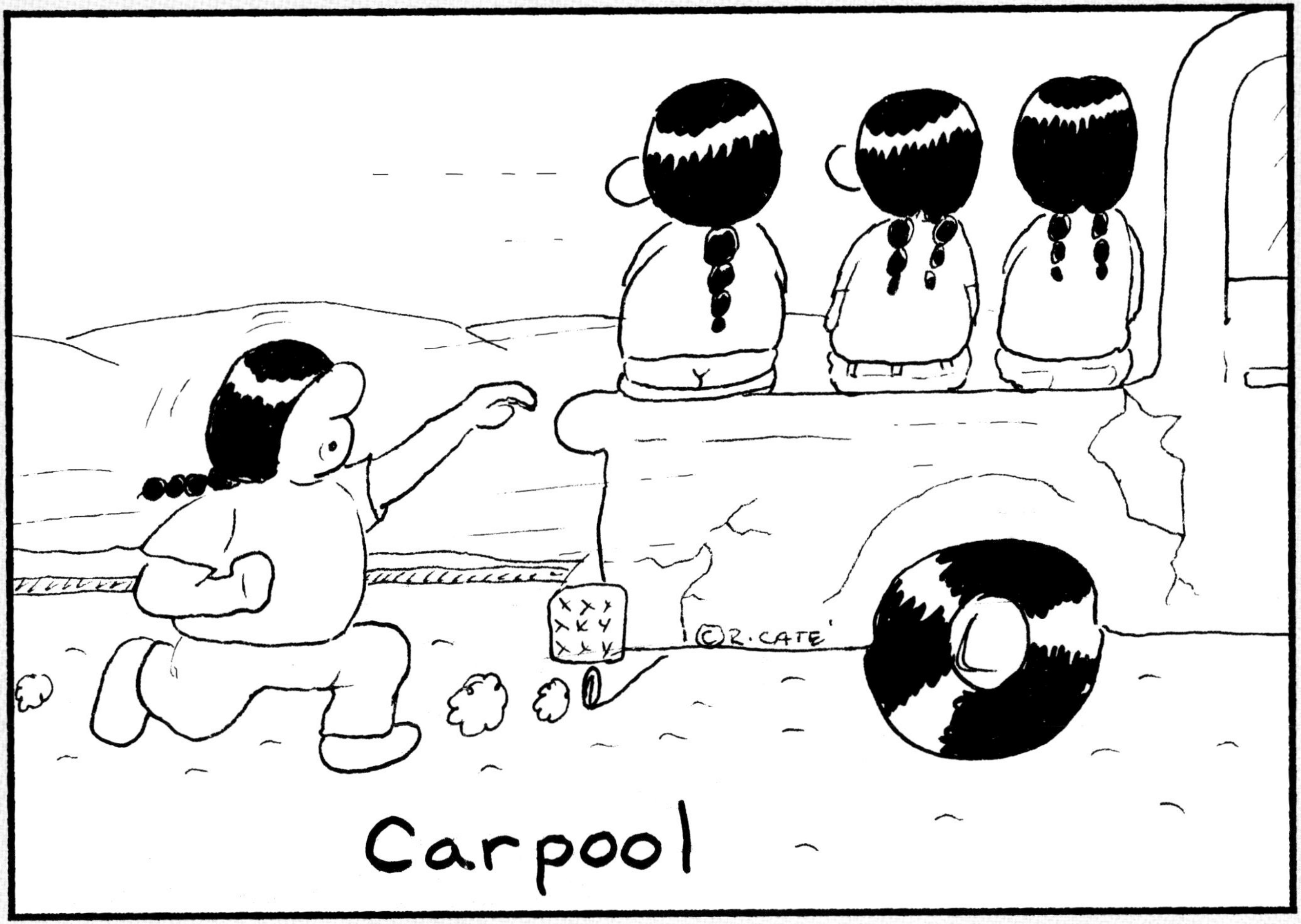
©R. CATE

Carpool

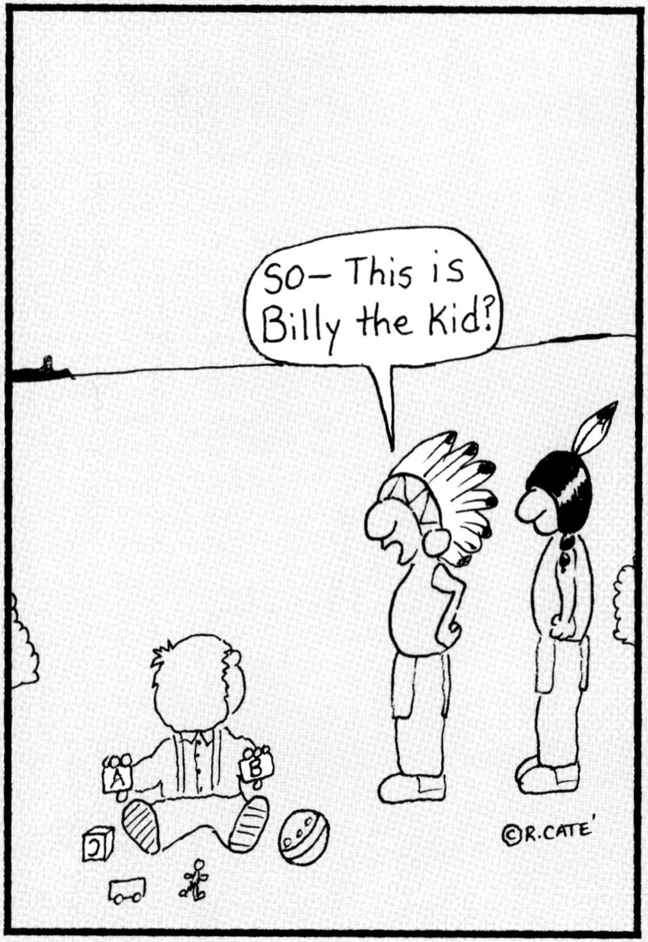
So– This is Billy the Kid?
A
B
©R.CATE'

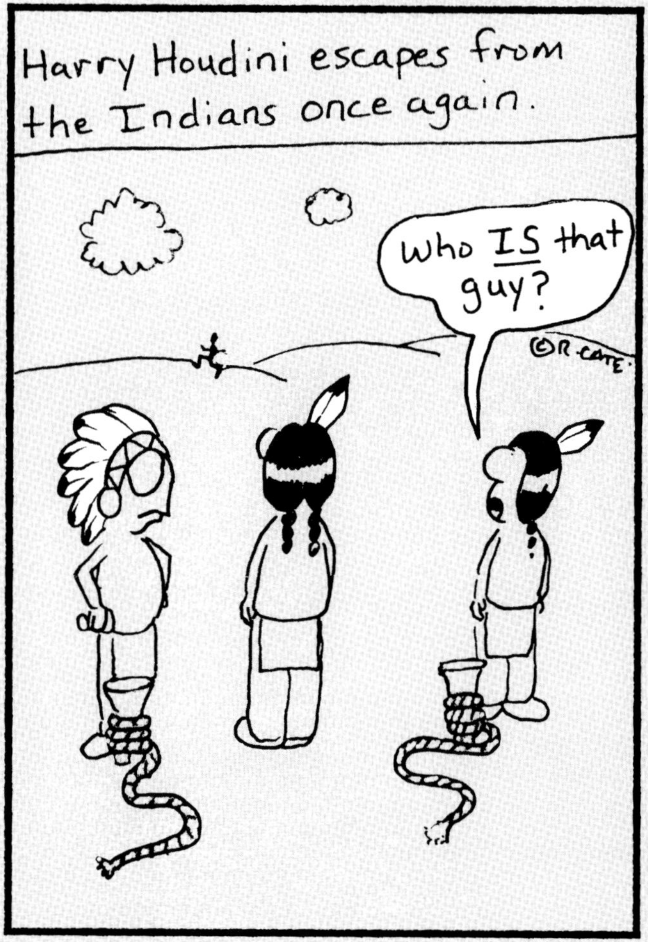
Harry Houdini escapes from the Indians once again.
Who IS that guy?
©R.CATE'

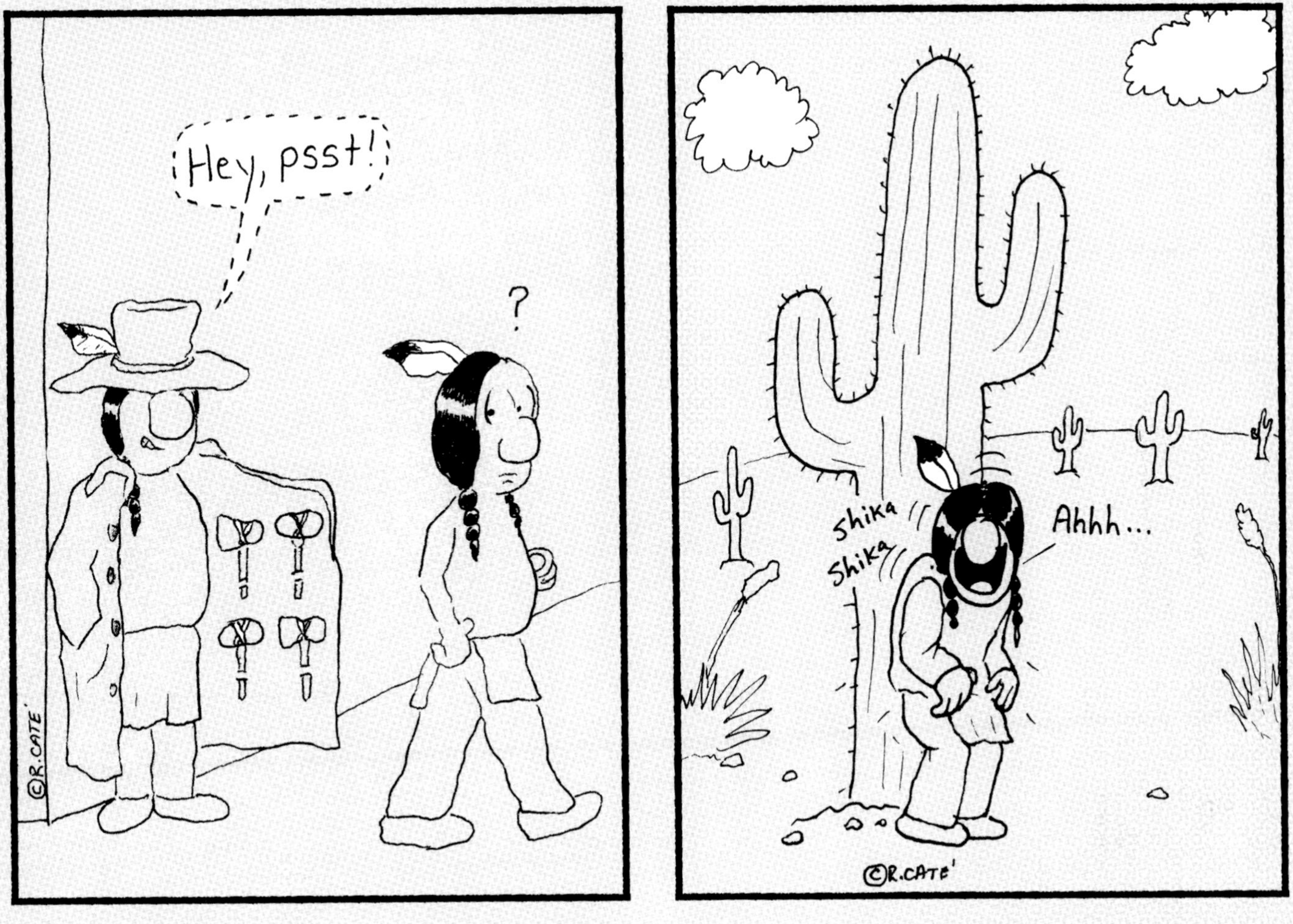
Hey, psst!
?
©R.CATE'
Shika Shika
Ahhh...
©R.CATE'

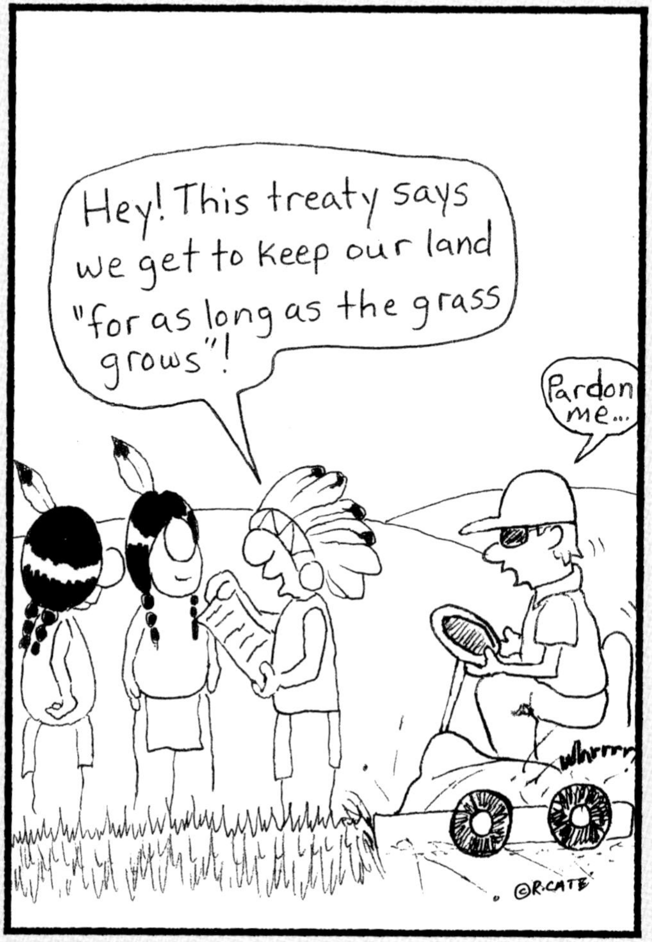
Hey! This treaty says we get to keep our land "for as long as the grass grows"!
Pardon me...
whrrrr
©R.CATE

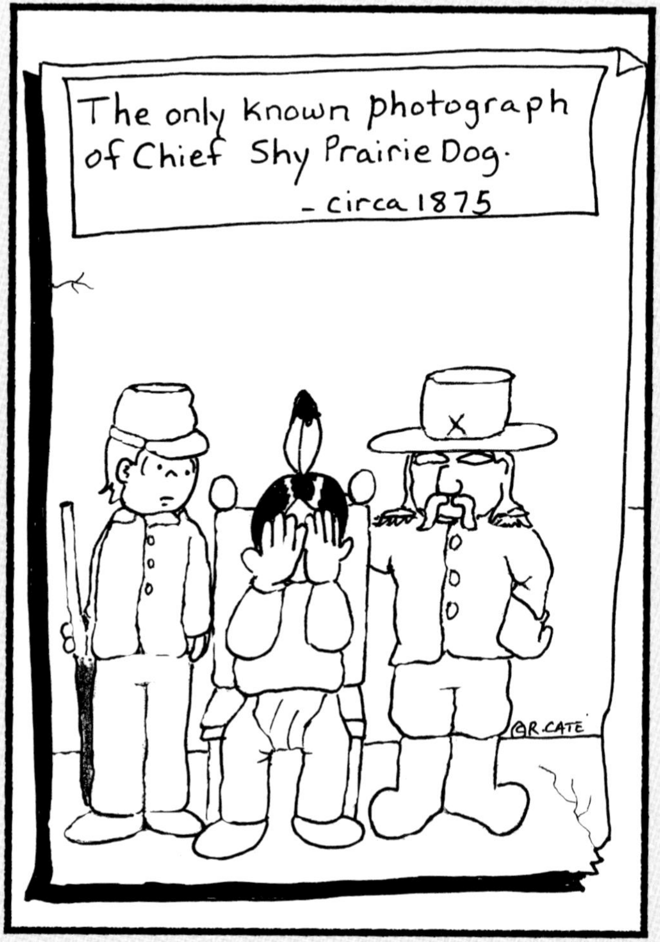
The only known photograph of Chief Shy Prairie Dog.
- circa 1875
©R.CATE

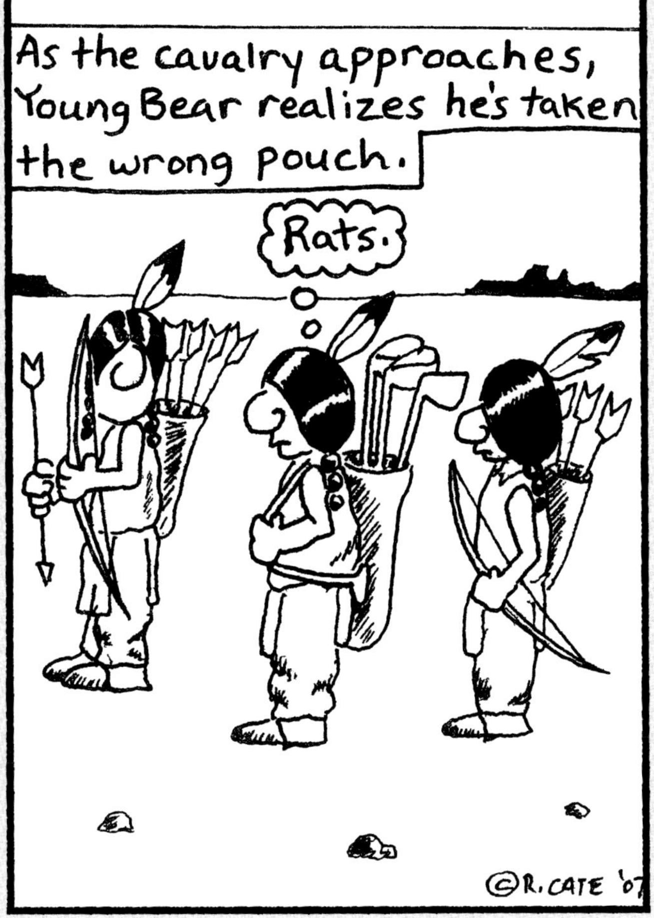

As the cavalry approaches, Young Bear realizes he's taken the wrong pouch.
Rats.
©R. CATE '07

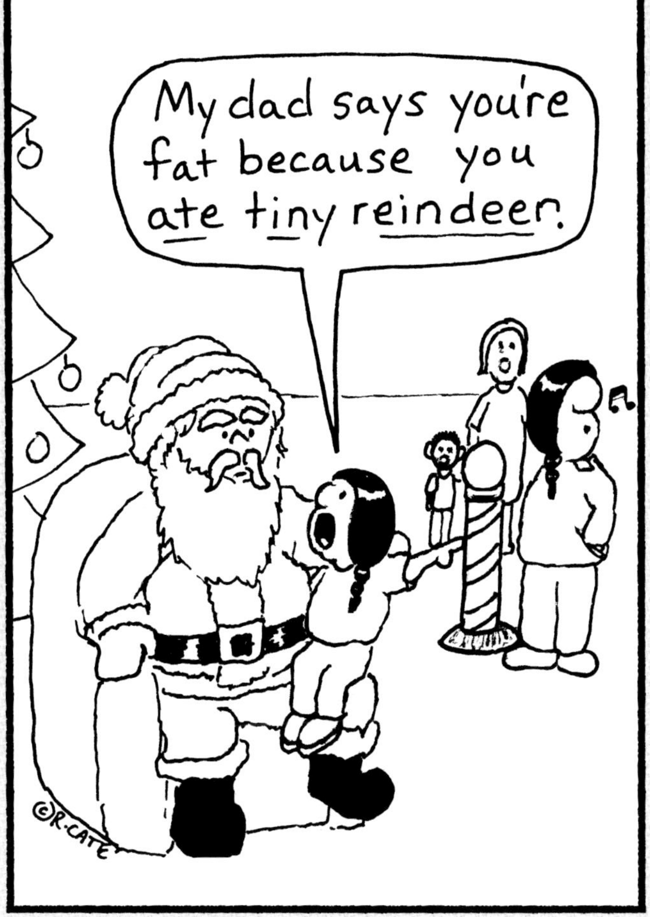

My dad says you're fat because you ate tiny reindeer.
©R-CATE

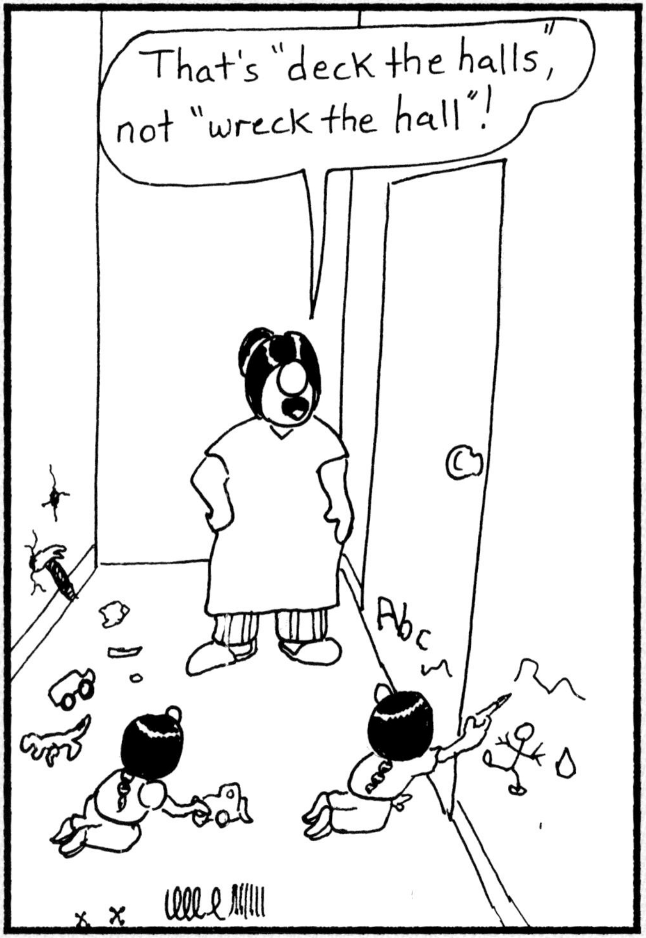
That's "deck the halls", not "wreck the hall"!
Abc

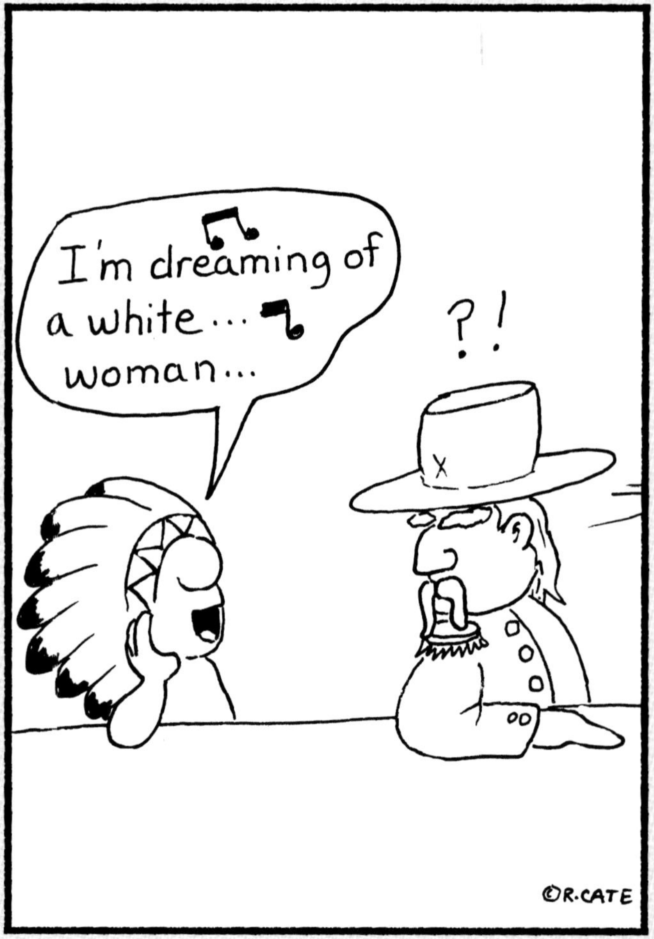
I'm dreaming of a white... woman...
?!
©R.CATE

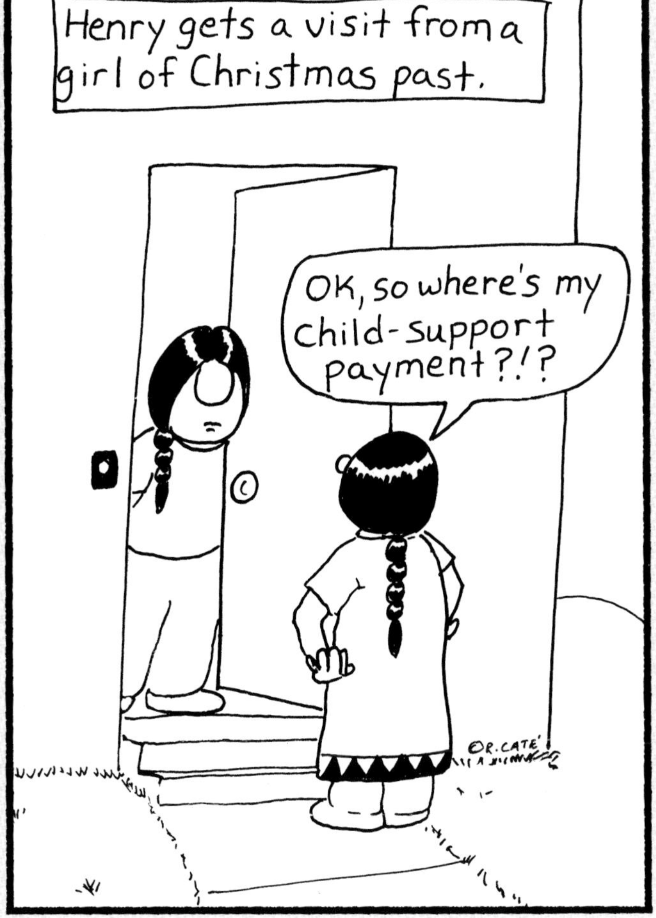
Henry gets a visit from a girl of Christmas past.
OK, so where's my child-support payment?!?
©R.CATE'

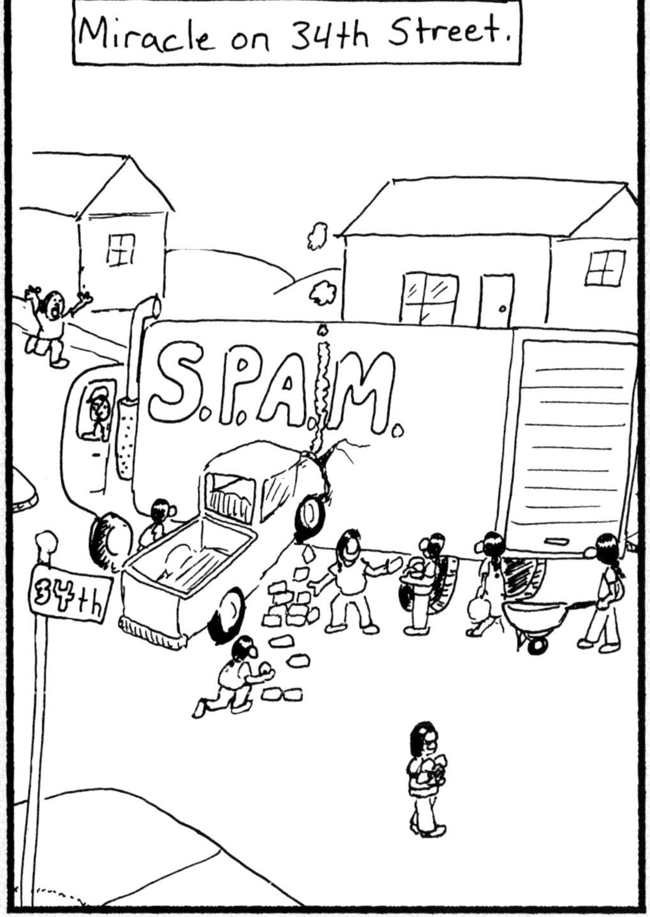
Miracle on 34th Street.
S.P.A.M.
34th

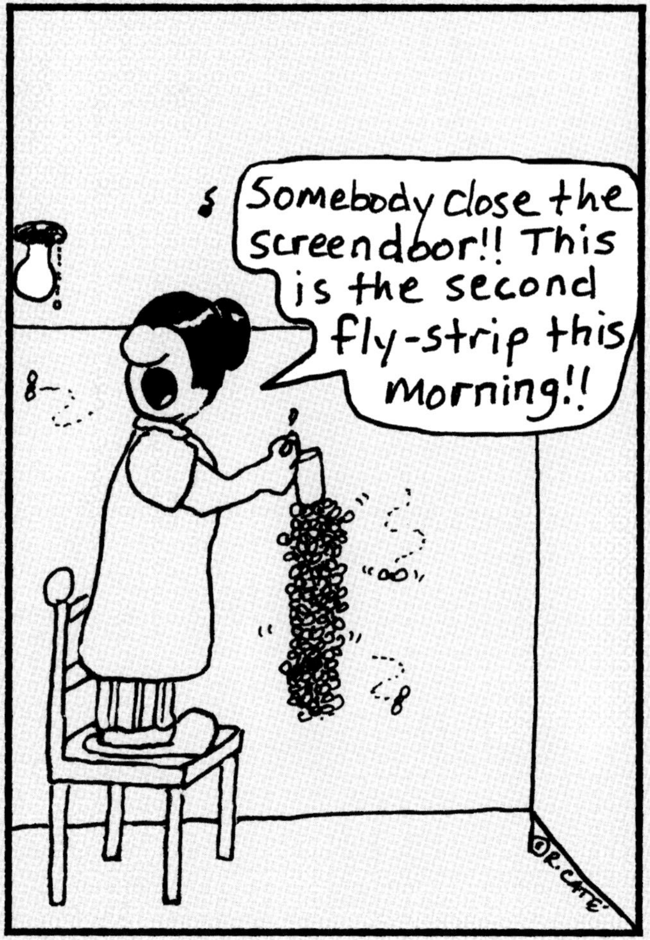
Somebody close the screendoor!! This is the second fly-strip this morning!!
©R.CATE'

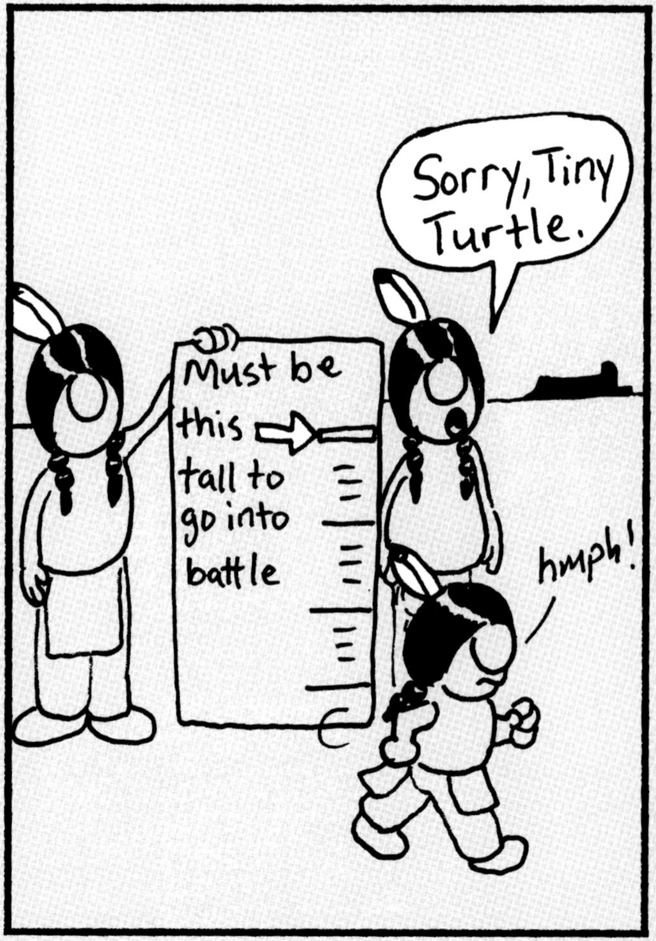
Sorry, Tiny Turtle.
Must be this tall to go into battle
hmph!

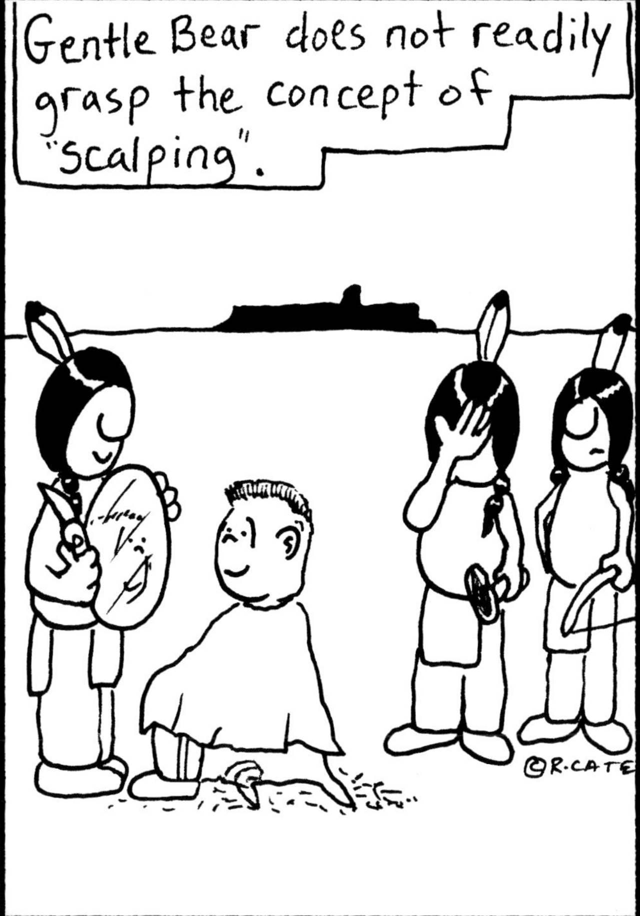
Gentle Bear does not readily grasp the concept of "scalping".
©R.CATE

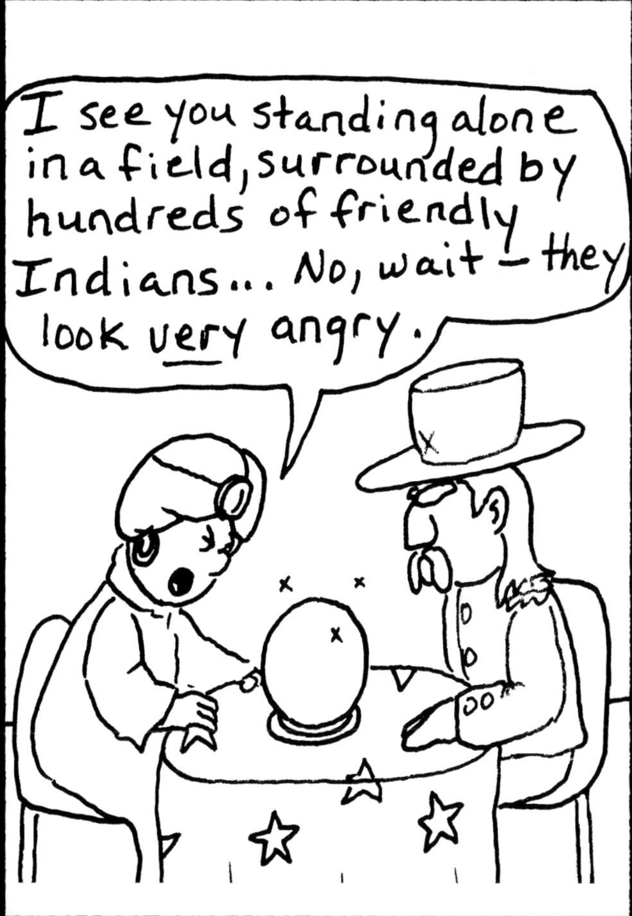
I see you standing alone in a field, surrounded by hundreds of friendly Indians... No, wait – they look very angry.

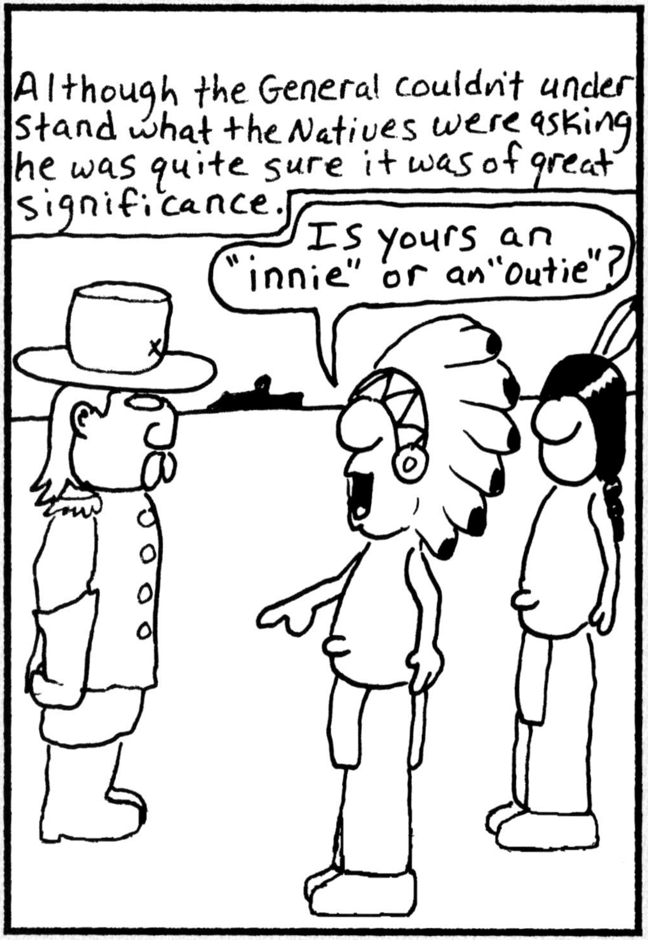
Although the General couldn't under stand what the Natives were asking he was quite sure it was of great significance.
Is yours an "innie" or an "outie"?

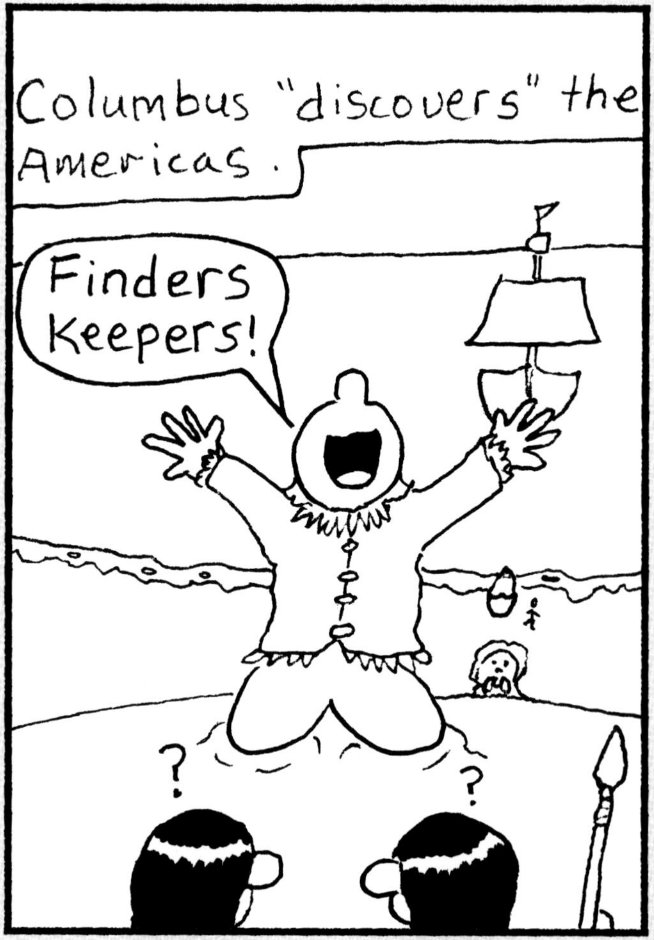
Columbus "discovers" the Americas.
Finders Keepers!
?
?

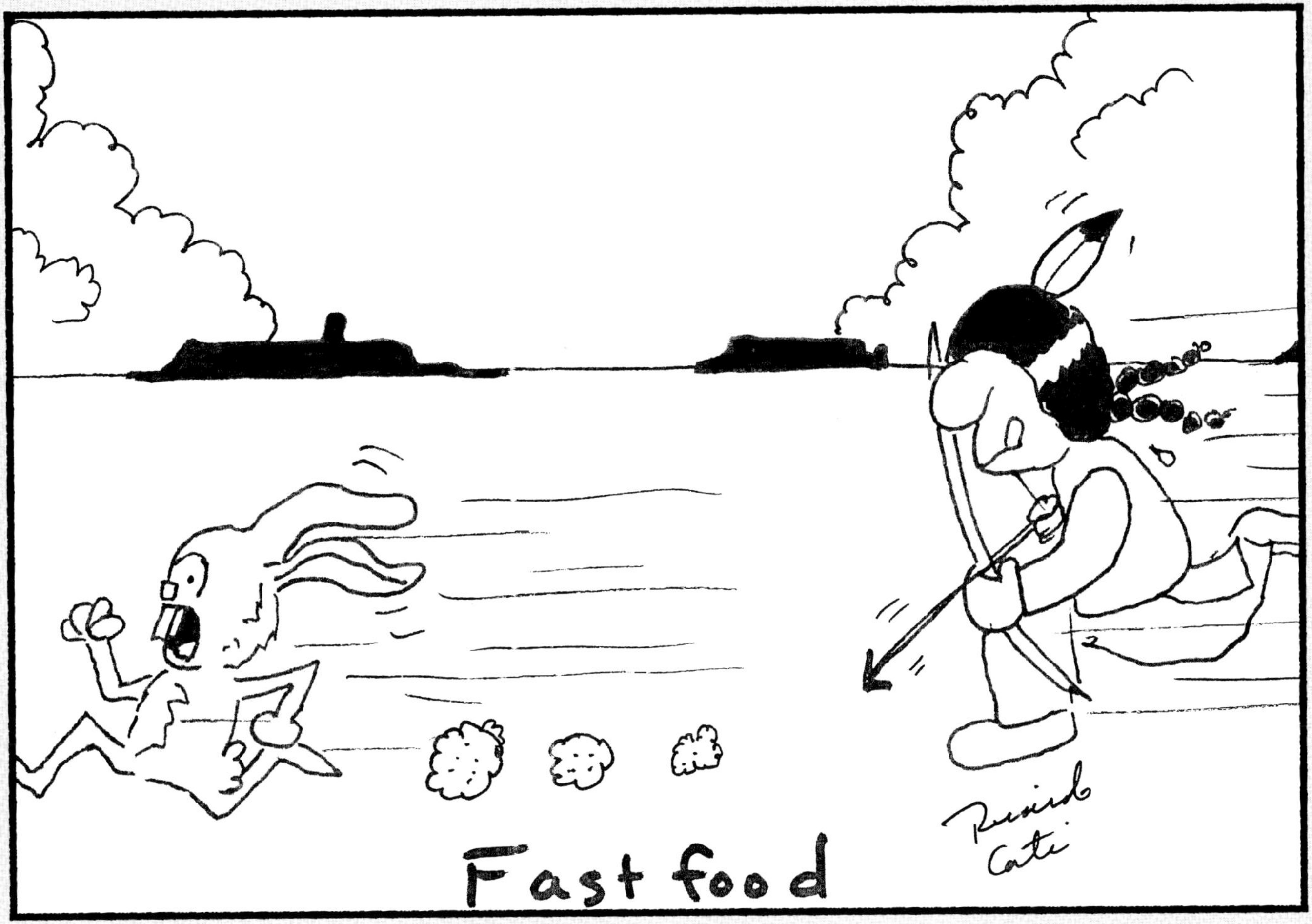
Fast food

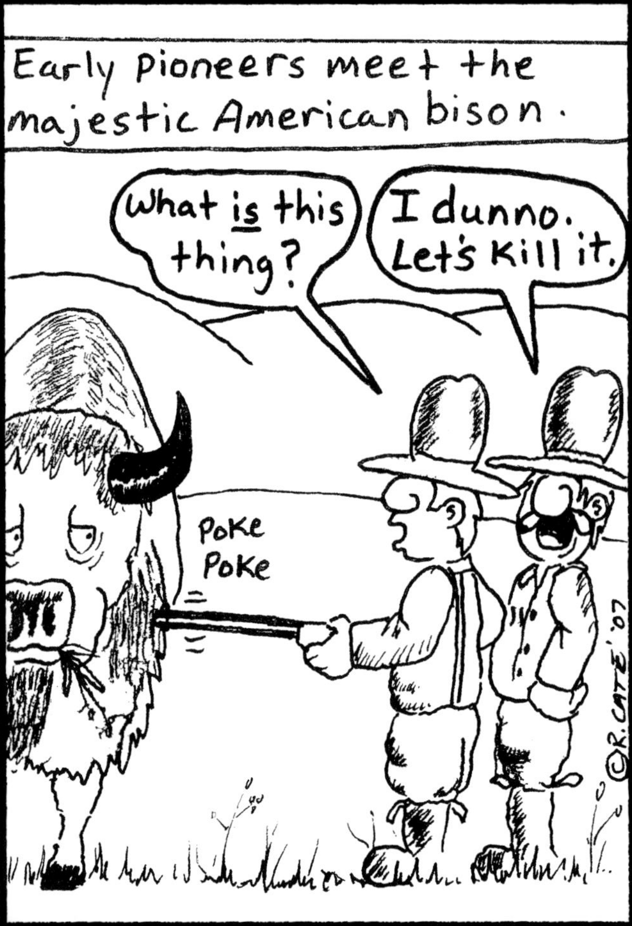
Early pioneers meet the majestic American bison.
What is this thing?
I dunno. Let's kill it.
Poke Poke
©R.CATE '07

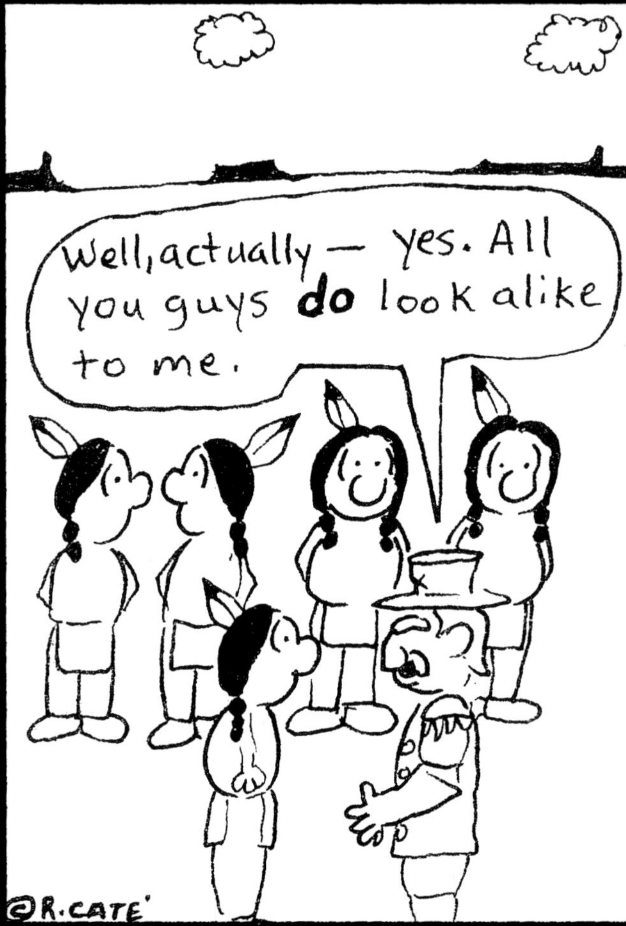
Well, actually — yes. All you guys do look alike to me.
©R.CATE

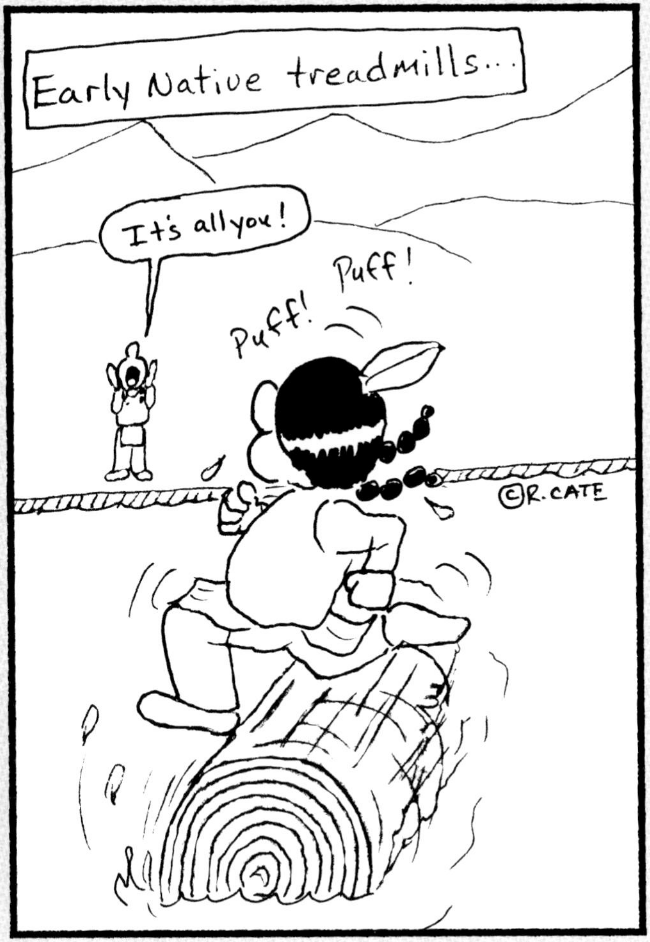
Early Native treadmills...
It's all you!
Puff!
Puff!
©R.CATE

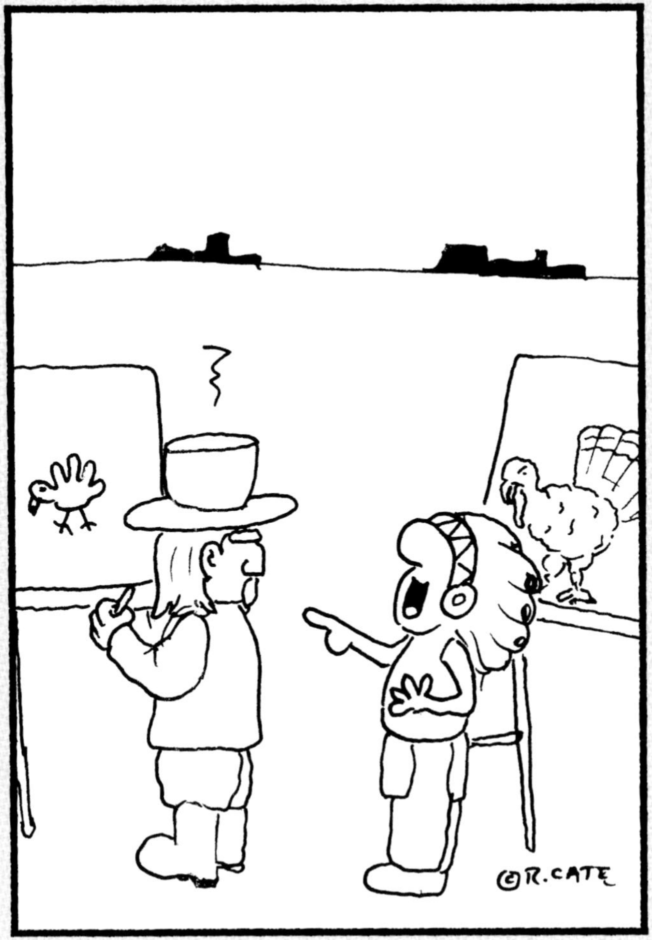
©R.CATE

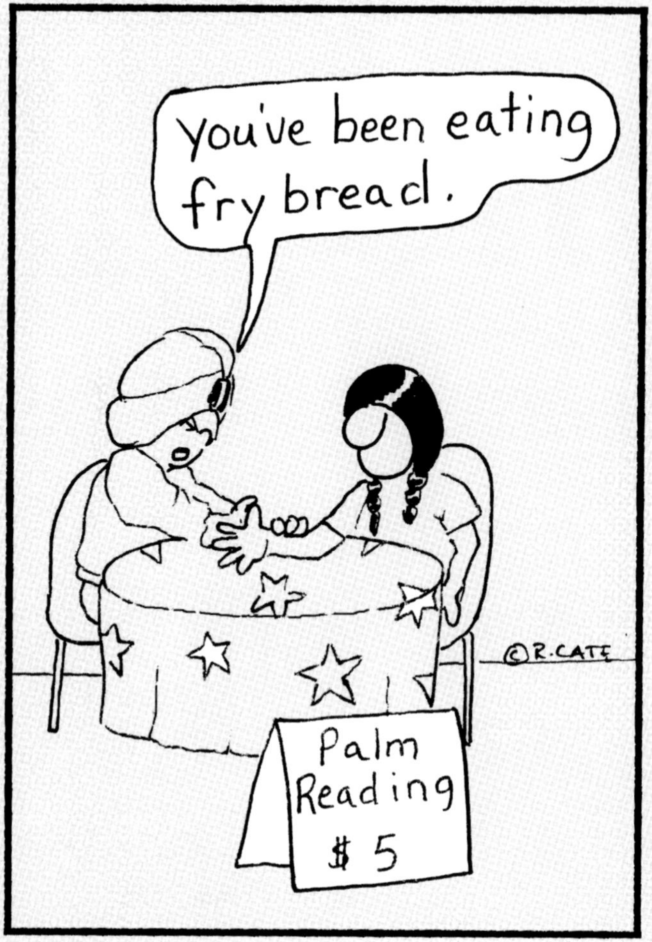
you've been eating fry bread.
Palm Reading $5
©R.CATE

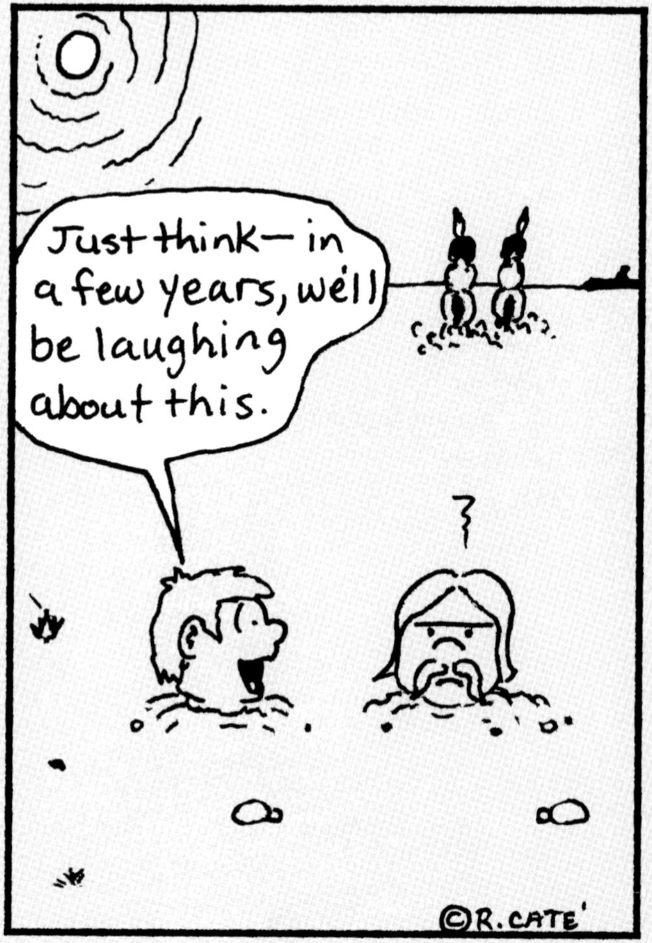
Just think—in a few years, we'll be laughing about this.
?
©R.CATE'